"Wonderful! Diane Frankenstein's book is a priceless gift to parents, teachers, and anyone who cares about children. Filled with wisdom, humor, helpful ideas—and most of all, the pure joy and passion for books—this volume is an absolute treasure. It is a great resource for everyone who loves children and books."

—T. A. Barron, author of *The Lost Years of Merlin*

"Diane Frankenstein has written an exceptional practical guide to exploring and expanding on children's literature that will help anyone who reads with children to extend the experience and help them make connections between their thoughts and what they read. Also, by enriching young readers' current experiences, it can encourage them to become lifelong readers drawn to the enduring power of the written word to help them understand and articulate thoughts about life as they experience it."

—Marie Conti, Senior Director of School Accreditation and Member Programs for the American Montessori Society

"In *Reading Together*, Frankenstein's enthusiasm for igniting children's love of reading is infectious. Her strategies are practical and actionable, and her book recommendations are a wonderful resource."

—Jeff Wetzler, Senior Vice President of Teacher Preparation, Support, and Development, and Chief Learning Officer of Teach for America

"In *Reading Together*, Diane Frankenstein provides a delightful springboard for conversations between adults and children about literature. The author distills a lifetime of reading and teaching children's literature into an accessible guidebook that will be useful in the library and the classroom and, most important, at home. Original and imaginative, the book is a wonderful resource for parents and educators who are interested in generating—and sustaining—a love of reading in young people."

—Coreen R. Hester, Head of School at the American School in London

"A must-have parenting tool! Diane's exceptional knowledge and experience in children's literature can finally be shared with the world. Parents and teachers from any culture will learn how to ignite a passion for reading in their children with this book. Offering over one hundred quality book recommendations, complete with related questions, this book will show you how to talk with children about books and the world we live in. Diane's reading tips and conversation starters can be used with any book, in any language!"

—Yolanda Yeh, Pro-Active Learning in Hong Kong

continued . . .

D0473433

"The subtitle of this book, *Everything You Need to Know to Raise a Child Who Loves to Read*, may sound audacious, but it's actually overly modest. Parents and educators who use this book will be raising children who love to learn. Diane Frankenstein teaches us that, through books, children learn language—oral and written—and through language, they learn to think. Importantly, she shows us that the most important outcome may not just be how many books children have read, but how many conversations they've had about them."

—Milton Chen, PhD, Executive Director of the George Lucas Educational Foundation

Reading Together

Everything You Need to Know to Raise a Child Who Loves to Read

DIANE W. FRANKENSTEIN

A PERIGEE BOOK

A PERIGEE BOOK
Published by the Penguin Group
Penguin Group (USA) Inc.
375 Hudson Street, New York, New York 10014, USA
Penguin Group (Canada), 90 Eglinton Avenue East, Suite 700, Toronto, Ontario M4P 2Y3, Canada
   (a division of Pearson Penguin Canada Inc.)
Penguin Books Ltd., 80 Strand, London WC2R 0RL, England
Penguin Group Ireland, 25 St. Stephen's Green, Dublin 2, Ireland (a division of Penguin Books Ltd.)
Penguin Group (Australia), 250 Camberwell Road, Camberwell, Victoria 3124, Australia
   (a division of Pearson Australia Group Pty. Ltd.)
Penguin Books India Pvt. Ltd., 11 Community Centre, Panchsheel Park, New Delhi—110 017, India
Penguin Group (NZ), 67 Apollo Drive, Rosedale, North Shore 0632, New Zealand (a division of Pearson
   New Zealand Ltd.)
Penguin Books (South Africa) (Pty.) Ltd., 24 Sturdee Avenue, Rosebank, Johannesburg 2196, South Africa

Penguin Books Ltd., Registered Offices: 80 Strand, London WC2R 0RL, England

While the author has made every effort to provide accurate telephone numbers and Internet addresses at the time of publication, neither the publisher nor the author assumes any responsibility for errors, or for changes that occur after publication. Further, the publisher does not have any control over and does not assume any responsibility for author or third-party websites or their content.

First edition: September 2009

Library of Congress Cataloging-in-Publication Data

Frankenstein, Diane Waxer.
  Reading together : everything you need to know to raise a child who loves to read /
Diane W. Frankenstein.— 1st ed.
      p.   cm.
  Includes bibliographical references and index.
  ISBN 978-0-399-53524-6
  1. Children—Books and reading—United States. 2. Reading—Parent participation. 3. Children's
literature—Bibliography. I. Title.
  Z1037.A1F7175 2009
  649'.58—dc22   2009016793

PRINTED IN THE UNITED STATES OF AMERICA

10 9 8 7 6 5 4 3

Most Perigee books are available at special quantity discounts for bulk purchases for sales promotions, premiums, fund-raising, or educational use. Special books, or book excerpts, can also be created to fit specific needs. For details, write: Special Markets, Penguin Group (USA) Inc., 375 Hudson Street, New York, New York 10014.

Contents

STORIES ARE ONE OF THE WAYS children try the world on for size. They help children find their place in the world. The best of stories show children who they are and as importantly, who they might become. *Reading Together* is dedicated to all children because, as the English poet Walter de le Mare described, "only the rarest kind of best in anything can be good enough for the young." This book is also dedicated to my sons, Daniel and Toby, my first audience—together we discovered a cache of stories. Early on I learned that we become the stories we read and the stories we tell and I saw how books truly make a difference in the life of a child. Even today, although my sons are now "all grown up," I find myself quoting from some of their favorite children's books of not so long ago. No one becomes too old for *The Little Engine That Could* or *Mike Mulligan and His Steam Shovel*, and children never outgrow the need for a little bit of humor, a little bit of encouragement, or a little bit of praise.

Introduction

Why I Read

The perennial child in me is always asking certain types of questions:

If I could take only one book with me to an island, which book would I take?

If I had to choose to live by the sea or in the mountains, which would I choose?

Is cherry pie really my most favorite pie? What about rhubarb pie?

So it comes as no surprise that I like the questions "Why do I like the books I like?" and "How did I become the reader I am today?" My answers are varied and take me from *The Arabian Nights*, a book I met when I was nine years old, to the advice Merlin gave Arthur in T. H. White's *Once and Future King*, to my admiration for the Talmudic tradition of Jewish learning, and last but not least, to the books of William Steig. I chuckle to think about the idiosyncratic path that led me to become the reader I am, and how it led me to discover the equation for getting children to love reading.

As a child I was seduced by the power of storytelling that came from reading Scheherazade's stories in *The Arabian Nights*. In the story, King Shahryar married and then executed each of his wives after a single night of marriage to make sure that his new wife would not stop loving him. Little did he know that when he married Scheherazade, she had a clever plan to save her life. Her nightly stories of Sinbad the Sailor and Ali Baba were so exciting that King Shahryar found himself postponing her execution again and again so he could hear the end of her story. At heart, we are all like King Shahryar, who fell under the spell of "Tell me more" and "Then what happened?" The essence of Scheherazade illustrates the transformative power of stories.

My curiosity and love of learning have been sustained by the advice Merlin gave Arthur in T. H. White's *Once and Future King*: "The best thing for being sad is to learn something. That's the only thing that never fails. You may grow old and trembling in your anatomies, you may lie awake at night listening to the disorder of your veins, you may miss your only love, you may see the world about you devastated by evil lunatics, or know your honour trampled in the sewers of baser minds. There is only one thing for it then—to learn." I can't count the number of times I have conjured up Merlin's advice, and it always proves true—learning is a wonderful antidote to life's doldrums and it keeps me alive to the wonders of the world.

My understanding of how children learn was influenced by Talmudic study, a fundamental element of Jewish education. Talmudic study has as its underlying principle the belief that individuals who study together—through questions and answers and conversations—are engaged in their learning, which makes learning relevant. This is how I came to understand that there is always more power in the questions than in the answers.

I will always remember the moment I met William Steig's *Gorky Rises*. My children were very small and I was astounded that such a book existed in the world of children's literature. Steig's books—in addition to having language that soared, pictures that captivated me, and stories I wanted to go on forever—showed me how distinctive and extraordinary children's books could be. I ravenously began to read all of his books, and I embarked on a mission to find other brilliant, amazing, and unforgettable books.

Because of my passion to read more children's books and wanting children to love reading as I did, I pursued a master's degree in children's literature and language arts. My graduate work primarily introduced me to the "usual suspects"—the "award winners"—and although these books are wonderful, I realized this was an incomplete list. I knew there had to be more, other books waiting to be read. It has been in my job as an educational consultant for the past twenty years to search for and discover these "other books" and share them with both adults and children.

In my classes and workshops, I introduce parents to the amazing and multifaceted world of children's literature, and I teach them how to help their children get more out of the books they read. In addition I consult with schools where I work with administrators, librarians, and faculty in developing dynamic and relevant literature components for their curricula. My work with children centers on helping them find what to read, and showing them how to get more from their reading experience and how to discover the excitement and pleasure that reading offers. I work primarily in the San Francisco Bay Area as well as nationwide and in Asia and Europe.

Early in my career as an educational consultant I believed that the key to turning children into readers was simply to put the right book in the right hands at the right time and, bingo, children would love the stories they read. I quickly realized that something was missing. I soon recognized children also needed to talk about the books they read. Showing children they have something to say about the books they read helps them engage and connect with a story— children who talk about stories understand the stories better. This is an essential component of children becoming confident readers, and children need confidence to be good readers. Every child needs and deserves the advantage of being a good reader.

What We Know About Children and Reading

Everyone likes stories, but not everyone loves to read. Many children are reluctant readers and find reading difficult and boring—something you do for a school assignment. They're not carrying the habit of reading for pleasure into their adolescence and young adulthood. Yet I'm willing to bet that many children who don't like reading have never found a book they liked and have never gotten beyond the plotline, which is just the beginning of the reading experience.

What do we know about children and reading? The most recent study to address the challenge of getting children to read comes from the 2008 Scholastic study "The Kids and Family Reading Report," which shows that "kids' reading drops off after eight years, and that parents can have a direct impact on getting kids to read ... When kids start reading independently, parents need to become more, not less, involved ... parents must play a key role in helping their older children select books that capture their imagination and interest ... Kids say that one of the main reasons why they do not read more is because they cannot find books that they like to read." Simply put? If pleasure doesn't drive reading, children don't become readers.

How do children become "good" readers? The challenge—getting children to read for pleasure—is obvious, but the solution has been to offer lists of recommended titles. A list of titles, while helpful, is not going to turn children into lovers of reading. So what do children need?

To begin, they need to read books that are appropriate in terms of reading level and emotional readiness, and this calls for the involvement of parents and the other adults in their lives to help them find the right book, their "home-run book"—a book that taps into their curiosity and interests, a book that makes them care about the characters and what happens to them. All children, even reluctant readers, become "good" readers when we offer them books they can read with enough ease to get into the story.

Children also need books that speak to their emotional maturity. What makes a child a "good" reader is comprehension and not what I call "barking at print." Offering children books that are beyond them in terms of reading ability and comprehension is a major reason why many children do not read for pleasure and see reading as a chore. When children tell me that a book is boring, it is often code for "I didn't get it." Children don't read critically and creatively at the same time, so when the reading level is too difficult or they are not yet developmentally ready for the story, they are not able to get to the story, and *children only read for story*.

In addition children need the adults in their lives to show them how to better understand and *make a story their own*. We best support them in this endeavor by having conversations that engage children in the stories they read.

When you put all these elements together, you're left with a winning equation:

Help children find an appropriate book

+ talk with them about the story

= children who connect with stories and love the stories they read

This winning equation creates children who read for pleasure and become lifelong lovers of reading. *Reading Together* is about this equation. In this book, you'll discover ways to help children find what to read and then, through conversation, show them how to find meaning and pleasure in their reading. Let there be no doubt: Children who get more from the books they read are children who love to read.

> **"**I suggest that the only books that influence us are those for which we are ready and which have gone a little further down our own particular path than we have yet gone ourselves.**"**
>
> —E. M. FORSTER, *TWO CHEERS FOR DEMOCRACY*

How to Help Children Love What They Read

The following guidelines are intended to support your efforts in creating readers who find both delight and surprise in the books they read. *Reading Together* is as much about *how* to read—and how to make sense of what you read—as *what* to read. The bottom line is that I want children to enjoy reading—no matter *what* they read. These guidelines grew out of many years of on-the-job reading with children, witnessing the idiosyncratic ways children read:

★ **Read what you love and love what you read.** Help your child find books and materials that tap into their interests. There is a sea of print out there—fiction, biography, nonfiction, essays, poetry, and so forth. Don't ignore any of them and also don't dismiss magazines, newspapers, manuals, graphic novels, and comic books. To read is to read!

★ **Read the right book at the right time.** Choose books that speak to both the appropriate reading level and a child's developmental readiness for the story. Children read for story and when they are working too hard with the mechanics of reading, it becomes difficult for them to enjoy the story. Let go of how easy or challenging a book may appear. Children want books they can understand.

★ **Keep the love of story alive.** While your child hones his[*] reading skills, encourage him to return to the picture books and early reads he loved when he was little—you are never too old to read a 32-page picture book! These are wonderful books to revisit and for older children to read on their own. They already have a love affair going!

★ **Help your child find the hook of the story—what taps into their curiosity and captures their interest quickly.** Children are not patient readers. They are not willing to read to page 50 to get hooked on a book. Give a book a fair chance and also let them know they don't have to finish or like every book. There is no reason why every child should like every book—it is all about the right book for the right child at the right time.

★ **Don't interrupt the reading of the story with explanations or editorials.** This gets in the way of the story and a child can easily become annoyed and frustrated with too many interruptions.

★ **Read the story as it is written.** Don't "monkey" with the way the story is written. Once you begin to tinker with the story, by substituting an easier word or leaving out complicated sentences or information that you think might be confusing, you are interfering with the magic of the story.

★ **Respect your child's taste.** Taste is personal and you may not like all the books your child chooses to read, but these are important books because they help your child hone her reading skills and build her confidence as a reader. Hang in long enough and you will see your child go from reading what you might call simplistic stories—those "okay reads"—to more challenging stories. Know your guidance is key in helping your child find books worth knowing with characters worth meeting.

★ **Keep the pleasure in reading.** *The Call of the Wild* in third grade may be a signal for *Balto and the Great Race*. If a book is too difficult, your child may better understand and enjoy the story if you read it to her out loud. Also encourage your child to read another book on their own for pleasure.

★ **Read aloud.** A child's desire to learn to read comes from being read to. Reading to your child taps into his imagination and curiosity and creates a love of story. Many of the skills children need to become good readers are first learned in the stories they hear.

[*]To avoid the awkward use of he or she, I alternate between both.

★ **Don't stop reading aloud to your children once they have mastered the ability to read on their own.** Some children, when they can read on their own, resist being read to—it can feel babyish. Reading aloud, sharing ideas, and talking about what matters to your child is not something that anyone outgrows. Be creative. Read something that will interest your child and keep alive the habit of reading together and sharing ideas. You are never too old to enjoy reading aloud.

★ **Don't turn reading into a vocabulary lesson.** Learning words in isolation gets in the way of comprehension and pleasure. If a child meets five or more words on a page that he doesn't know and can't figure out, he is probably on the young side for that particular book. Don't push—come back to the book at a future time.

★ **Have books in places where they will be easy to pick up.** Is there a room in your house that does not have books? Why doesn't it?

★ **Slow down.** Encourage your child to read fewer books and know them well. Children need comprehension not speed to be good readers. Too many people find themselves on literary StairMasters, moving fast but going nowhere.

★ **Encourage your child to read a book more than once.** When you first read a book you are following the basic plotline. A second read delivers different pleasures by allowing you the opportunity to pick up the subtleties and nuances of the story that are often missed on a first read.

★ **Audio books (*not* the abridged stories) are terrific.** Listening to books on tape is not cheating! Don't relegate audio books only to long car rides. Audio books are another wonderful way to increase the stories children have in their memory banks. An added bonus—audio books build vocabulary!

★ **Be creative and find other times in a day—not just bedtime—when reading can happen.** Bedtime reading is wonderful but is not the *only* time of the day to read. At the end of the day children and parents are tired, and the last time I checked, tired and cranky and a short attention span all go hand in hand. How about a poem with breakfast? How about a short story with a snack? How about one chapter with dessert at dinner?

★ **Expect your children to love reading.** The Michigan Department of Education conducted a survey and found that more than budgets or teachers, parents are the reason children perform as they do in school, and the most consistent predictors of children's academic achievement and social adjustment are parental expectations. Expect your children to love reading and support that expectation by helping them find their home-run books.

> **"** 'What is the use of a book,' thought Alice, 'without pictures or conversations?' **"**
>
> —LEWIS CARROLL, *ALICE'S ADVENTURES IN WONDERLAND*

The Art of Conversational Reading

Read a book—ask a question—start a conversation. This is the essence of *Reading Together*. Nobody comes into the world knowing how to talk about a story. Finding meaning in a story calls for guessing, speculation, and pondering; it's less about what *you know* and more about what *you think*. It's a little like thinking out loud. I call this skill conversational reading, which is less about trying to figure out the meaning of the stories and more about what the story means to children in their lives now.

Most children thrive on questions; it's as if they breathe out question marks as they try the world on for size. Parents want to have good conversations with their children but the reality is that while parents often think they know many of the answers, a good conversation is *not* about the answers, it is about the questions.

At heart, conversational reading is making comments and asking questions—it is talking with children about the stories they read. Conversational reading encourages a reader to linger, saunter, and contemplate a story; metaphorically speaking, it is shining a flashlight into a dark cave and saying, "Did you notice that?" and "Look over there." Conversational reading helps children develop the ability to use words to express themselves and gives them a command of language. Children who talk about stories and the subjects a story explores better understand what they read. Children who better understand stories become more confident readers, and this confidence directly impacts the pleasure children find in the stories they read.

To practice conversational reading, keep the following tips in mind:

★ **Start a conversation with a good question.** A good question is a question that takes you someplace in your thinking. Children learn more by looking for the answer to a question and not finding it than they do from learning the answer itself. The best questions to begin with are "What do you notice?" and "What do you think?"

★ **Start your conversation with the reader's interest.** The best books are always about more than one subject, so when starting a conversation try to gauge your child's particular interest in the story.

★ **To begin a conversation, ask specific, concrete questions—where the answers can be found inside the story.** Concrete questions help children make sense of the story. For example: Q: "Why does Hunter cut up his frog?" A: "Because Stripe told him to." Beginning a conversation with "What's the meaning of the story?" could puzzle and frustrate children. A child needs to understand the story before she can begin to understand *the meaning* of the story.

★ **Once the conversation gets moving, help your child see beyond the plotline.** When you can't see beyond the plotline of a story the story forever remains one-dimensional. For example in *Bargain for Frances*, the plot centers on Thelma tricking Frances into buying her tea set, but once you get beyond this basic plotline, you begin to understand that the story is also about friendship, doing the right thing, being easily influenced, and fairness. It is not just a story about tea sets!

★ **Rephrase questions.** Often a child can't respond to a question because the question does not make sense. Ask the same questions but use different words. "How would you describe Dominic?" can feel abstract whereas "What words describe Dominic—*adventurous, generous, curious, kind, empathetic, smart, independent, fair, noble*?" will be easier for children to answer.

★ **Be realistic about your expectations for the conversation.** A conversation is not a literary discussion. The conversation could be as simple as "I wish I had a backpack like Hunter's" (*Hunter's Best Friend at School*) to "Why did Derek steal the jewels?" (*The Real Thief*).

★ **Offer what you think, too.** Be willing to offer what you think to get the conversation started. Make the distinction—a conversation is less about what *you know* and more about what *you think*.

★ **Make personal connections to a story.** "Has this ever happened to you?" "What would you do in this situation?" "Does the main character remind you of anyone you know?" Conversations that move away from the plotline and into the personal are how children see connections between a story and their lives.

★ **Be patient.** It takes time to learn how to have a conversation about a story that doesn't sink the story with too many comments and questions. You will find your rhythm and discover the ebb and flow of conversations.

★ **Try listening.** If you ask children a question, you have to wait a little while and allow them to think and respond. Ask one question, make one comment, and *wait*. Don't underestimate the importance of showing your child you are listening and hearing what he says.

★ **Keep the conversation moving.** A conversation can feel a little like being caught in traffic—you want to keep everyone moving and avoid chaos. Pay attention to who has the right of way and who needs to yield. Phrases that help keep ideas moving include "Why do you say that?" "Are you saying . . . ?" "That is interesting. Can you tell me more?" and "Why do you think that?"

★ **Avoid hijacking the conversation.** Proceed with caution and keep front and center: A conversation is a dialogue, not a monologue.

★ **You don't need to agree.** Don't get stuck on one-way streets. One-way streets only take you in one direction and are not as interesting as two-way streets. At the end of the day, there are no right answers in a conversation. Conversations are meant to give a greater understanding of different views and perspectives, not necessarily to reach a resolution.

★ **"What if" is a powerful tool to get your imagination working.** Conversational reading promotes looking at a story from different perspectives. Imagine how another character might tell the story.

★ **Use genuine puzzlement and a spirit of wonder to drive a conversation.** Comments and questions, driven by a spirit of wonder and puzzlement, capture a child's curiosity. "Why do you think the chicken crossed the road?" yields a different conversation than "How many times did the chicken cross the road?"

★ **Don't settle for the obvious.** Conversational reading grows the habit of mindfulness and makes it difficult to settle for the quick and obvious response. This is how children develop critical thinking skills.

★ **Follow Winnie the Pooh's advice on conversation:** "It is more fun to talk with someone who doesn't use long, difficult words but rather short, easy words like 'what about lunch?'"

> **"**Man's mind, once stretched by a new idea, never regains its original dimensions.**"**
>
> —OLIVER WENDELL HOLMES

Why I Chose These Books

In this guide, you'll find 101 books to explore with your child. With so many available books why did I choose these particular 101 books? *Reading Together* is not a textbook on children's literature, and I don't mean to suggest these are the only books that matter. My selection of books comes from my classes and workshops for children, parents, and teachers. My choices were predicated on my belief that books are both windows and mirrors. Windows, because they are one of the ways children extend their knowledge of the world, and mirrors, because they are one of the ways children come to understand themselves. These stories do not minimize, dumb down, or patronize the challenges children face or the emotions they feel. The titles in *Reading Together* respect children and offer stories that are diverse and are not of one mind or one perspective. They were selected based on story, literary merit, and the conversations they jumpstart. Ultimately my choices were inspired by the wisdom from one of my favorite writers, Isaac Bashevis Singer, who wrote for both children and adults. In his speech "Why I Write for Children," delivered on the occasion of his acceptance of the National Book Award in 1970, he said, "[Children] love interesting stories, not commentary, guides, or footnotes. When a book is boring, they yawn openly, without any shame or fear of authority." These 101 notable books are some of my favorites and I hope that many of them become your child's favorites as well. I made every effort to use books that are still in print, but there may be a few you will have to find at your library.

Why You Need This Book

Parents and teachers are the busiest people on earth. Turning children into life-time readers calls for teamwork on the part of *all* the adults in the life of a child—family, caregivers, teachers, and librarians—to help children find their home-run books. Teachers are trained to teach children how to read, and *all* the adults in the life of a child have the opportunity to show that child *how to love reading* by helping him find great stories, and through questions that jump-start conversations, show him how to mine a story for its treasures. The books in *Reading Together* offer stories on subjects that are important to children and the conversations that these books jump-start allow children to better understand what they read. Show them your passion for a story and see how your passion becomes contagious. Don't waste precious time trying to convince your child of the importance of reading—just read him good stories.

Although the books in *Reading Together* are recommended for children in grades pre-K through six and up, the Look Closer questions on the Story Pages and the Subject Conversation questions work for adolescents as well. When your adolescent tells you it's not necessary to talk—and they say, "I know that!'—it's especially important to have those conversations. Don't let go of the earlier habit of talking with your child and sharing ideas. Parents need to be *more involved* with their preteen children and these two sets of questions give parents what they need to jump-start those much-needed conversations. In our fast-moving, media-saturated world, thoughtful conversations are more important than ever before.

How to Use This Book

Part I consists of the 101 Story Pages. In addition, you'll find "Conversation Starters for Any Story." These questions can be asked for any story and aren't specific to any one book. Also included is "The Key to the Story Pages," which explain the elements on each of the Story Pages. The 101 Story Pages are divided into three categories—picture books, books for children in grades 2 to 5, and books for children in grades 4 to 6 and up—that easily guide you to grade-appropriate books.

The + sign following a grade level (5+) indicates that this book is recommended for that grade and beyond. Some of the books might feel young in terms of reading level for their respective categories but I rarely meet a child who comes to a book too late. Connecting a child to the right book at the right time depends not just on the appropriate reading level but also on the emotional readiness a child brings to their reading. The recommended grade levels are only suggestions—a child's preference and readiness are the real measures and ultimately the deciding factors. In addition, each Story Page suggests the grade levels at which the books can be read together or read alone. A read-aloud experience is completely different from a book a child reads on her own. Each Story Page offers a brief book synopsis providing a peek into the plot to draw you into the story. The synopsis also highlights some of the subjects found in the stories so that you can easily find a book that taps into an interest or subject your child may want to talk about—these range from friendship and envy to doing the right thing. On each Story Page, there are two types of questions and every question can become a conversation.

Who, What, Where, and Why questions jump-start conversations to help your child understand the plot of the story: "What makes Peggy popular?" "How does Hunter help Stripe be his best self?" Concrete questions help children make sense of a story and build comprehension. To avoid making your child feel he is in the middle of a quiz, the questions often contain a partial answer that begins a conversation. The last thing you want is for your child to feel this is an exercise in reading comprehension. The questions have a contemplative tone and the conversations they jump-start encourage reflection—this is all about the conversations, not about questions and answers. The purpose is to make talking about a story a habit—talk is essential and the more meaningful and substantive the better.

The second type of question—the Look Closer questions—spark conversations that move from the plot to the personal: "What would you do in this situation?" "Which character do you like or dislike?" These questions take you deeper into the story and are how children see connections between the stories they read and their lives.

Each Story Page also offers a Souvenir—an idea you want to remember from the story—as well as What I Noticed—a section that offers, "This is what I noticed when the story ended," and asks, "What did you notice when the story ended?" In addition, you'll find a Next box with a list of suggested books. When a child reaches the end of a well-loved book, you often hear, "I want another book just like the one I just finished." To satisfy that request there are additional book recommendations that tap into their enthusiasm for the book they just finished. The books listed in the Next box connect either by tone, story line, or a subject found in the story. Along with new titles, I purposely suggested titles from the 101 books to make it easy for parents to find books on similar subjects that already provide the questions for conversations. Each Story Page provides what you need to help your child enjoy and get the most from the books she reads.

Part II features Subject Conversations. These are questions on some of the many challenges of childhood that parents want to help their children understand. Talking about what matters to children, whether it be inside a story (questions on the Story Pages) or outside a story (questions on the Subject Conversation pages), gives children the language they need to shape their thinking—it teaches them how to think. As E. M. Forster said, "How can I know what I think till I see what I say?"

If the Subject Conversations start your child thinking on a subject, the story conversations allow him to *experience* the subject *through the story*. A conversation on the subject of popularity and a conversation on a particular story where popularity is a topic yield two very different conversations. Moving freely between the two gives your child more to think about and more to talk about, which results in more thoughtful conversations. My advice is to use the Subject Conversations and the conversations on the Story Pages together to build conversations that are richer and more satisfying.

You can use the elements in *Reading Together* in a number of ways . . . in other words, whatever works best for you:

★ Choose a book from the Story Pages and find questions that prompt conversations to help your child get more from a story.

★ Select a question from the Subject Conversation section. These questions are organized by subject and allow you to quickly get to the conversation.

★ Use the questions on the Story Pages and the questions on the Subject Conversation pages together—when combined they offer a broad choice of questions that move a conversation in many different directions.

Now, let's start reading!

PART I

101 Story Pages

> " The answers aren't important really ... What's
> important is—knowing all the questions. "
>
> —ZILPHA KEATLEY SNYDER, *CHANGELING*

Conversation Starters for Any Story

While each Story Page provides questions to get a conversation started, you can also sprinkle in a few of the questions below in a chatty manner so your child does not feel that you are looking for a specific answer or that you are putting him or her on the spot. These general conversation-starter questions will work with any story every time. And all you need is one really good question to jump-start a really good conversation.

Conversation Starters

☆ Tell the story just by looking at the pictures.

☆ What on the first page keeps you reading?

☆ Which character are you most curious about?

☆ Tell me the story in your own words.

☆ How do the characters change from the beginning of the story to the end?

☆ Which character changes most in the story?

☆ Which character has not changed?

☆ How would the story be different if . . . ?

☆ Which character would you want to be your friend?

☆ Is there a character you dislike?

☆ If you could invite one character to dinner, who would it be?

☆ Who is the most important character in the story?

☆ Who is telling the story? How would another character tell the story?

☆ How would the story be different if a girl or a boy told the story?

☆ What would you do in this situation?

☆ What title would you give the story?

☆ Using only eight words, what is the plot of this story?

☆ Do you like the ending of the story? If not, how would you end the story?

☆ Does the ending fit the story?

☆ Does the story call for a sequel? (What are some of your favorite books that called for a sequel but did not deliver one?)

☆ What other books does this story make you think of?

☆ What are you curious about at the end of the story?

The Key to the Story Pages

Each Story Page includes the following elements:

 World of Ideas: A list of subjects this story explores.

 Story Synopsis: A brief summary that draws you into a story by giving you a peek at the plot.

 Who, What, When, and Why: The desire to find out—who, what, when, and why—keeps the pages turning. These questions jump-start conversations to help you understand the story.

 Look Closer: These questions help move the conversation from the plot to the personal.

 Souvenir: A quote from the story you want to remember . . . consider asking your child what souvenir he or she would choose.

 What I Noticed: This section offers, "This is what I noticed when the story ended." And it asks, "What did you notice when the story ended?"

 Quotes: An outside quote to extend your thinking about the story.

 Next?: One book leads to another . . . If your child liked this story, here are some further suggestions.

PICTURE BOOKS

BOOKS FOR CHILDREN IN GRADES 2 to 5

BOOKS FOR CHILDREN IN GRADES 4 to 6+

Amos and Boris

William Steig

WORLD OF IDEAS

Adventure, curiosity, differences, gratitude, making a difference, reciprocity

Story Synopsis

A heartwarming tale of friendship and adventure. Amos, a curious and adventurous mouse, sets out on a sailing adventure only to find himself adrift in the immense ocean with no land in sight. Drowning in the ocean, Amos is befriended and saved by a big whale named Boris. Years later Amos gets a chance to reciprocate Boris's good deed in an equally unlikely situation.

Who, What, When, and Why

★ Why does Amos build a boat? What is he curious about?
What does he name his boat? Why does he give his boat that name?
What provisions does he take on his journey? What would you take on a journey?

★ What does Amos like about his journey? What are some of the sights he sees on his ocean voyage?

★ Where is Boris going when he spots Amos in the ocean?
Boris says he is a mammal. Is a whale a fish or a mammal?

★ Why can't Boris and Amos meet again if they are such good friends?

READING TOGETHER

READ TOGETHER: GRADE PRE-K–2
READ ALONE: GRADE 1–3

Look Closer

☆ Amos is both curious and adventurous, and he builds a boat by himself and ventures out to explore the world. Are you adventurous? What are you curious about?

☆ Do only big gestures make a difference in someone's life? Can small gestures make a difference in someone's life, such as offering someone a smile, doing someone a favor, or offering them a cookie? How could you make a difference in someone's life?

☆ How important is it to let someone know when you are thankful for something?

Souvenir

"Much as he wants to do something, what can such a little fellow do?"

What I Noticed

Both Amos and Boris showed me how important it is to show your gratitude and, whenever possible, return a good deed.

What did you notice?

 Quotes

"You don't have to be big to be great."
—SHALOM ALEICHEM

Next

Check out these other titles:

Aesop's Fables,
specifically "Lion and the Mouse"
BY CAROL WATSON

Just So Stories
BY RUDYARD KIPLING

The Old Woman Who Named Things
BY CYNTHIA RYLANT

Owen and Mzee
BY ISABELLA HATKOFF

The Snail and the Whale
BY JULIA DONALDSON

That's What Friends Are For
BY FLORENCE PARRY HEIDE

Angelo

David Macaulay

WORLD OF IDEAS

Compassion, death, encouragement, making a difference, open-mindedness, responsibility, unlikely friendship

Story Synopsis

Angelo is an Italian craftsman who restores ancient Roman buildings and is not a big fan of pigeons. One day he finds a nest with an injured baby pigeon named Sylvia and takes her home to convalesce. An unlikely friendship grows as he cares and restores Sylvia to health.

Who, What, When, and Why

★ Angelo doesn't like pigeons. Why does he take the pigeon home?
  Would you have taken the pigeon home? What would your parents say?

★ What makes Angelo go from not liking pigeons to becoming good friends with a pigeon?
  Why does he decide the pigeon needs a name?

★ What does Angelo do to help Sylvia recover her health?
  Why does Angelo feel he needs to find Sylvia a home?

★ How does Sylvia help Angelo?

READ TOGETHER: GRADES PRE-K–2
READ ALONE: GRADES 1–3

 Look Closer

☆ Have you ever disliked someone and then, when you got to know them, liked them?

☆ Does the story have a happy or sad ending? What makes the ending sad? What makes the ending happy? Can a story be both sad and happy?
Can you remember a time you felt both happy and sad at the same time?

Souvenir

"She was just beginning her career in the performing arts—as an actress in one of the more popular piazzas."

What I Noticed

I loved that Sylvia made Angelo's hat part of her nest.

What did you notice?

 Quotes

"Still—in a way—nobody sees a flower—really—it is so small, we haven't time—and to see takes time, like to have a friend takes time."
—GEORGIA O'KEEFE

Next

Check out these other titles:

A Visitor for Bear
BY BONNY BECKER

Bently and egg
BY WILLIAM JOYCE

Dog and Bear
BY LAURA VACARO SEEGER

Fly High Fly Low
BY DON FREEMAN

How to Heal a Broken Wing
BY BOB GRAHAM

The Old Woman Who Named Things
BY CYNTHIA RYLANT

Rose Meets Mr. Wintergarten
BY BOB GRAHAM

A Bad Case of Stripes

David Shannon

WORLD OF IDEAS

Being honest with yourself,
conformity,
fitting in, integrity,
wanting to impress

Story Synopsis

Camilla Cream develops a bad case of stripes from fretting about what to wear on the first day of school. Camilla was always worried about what other people thought of her, until the day arrived when she no longer recognized herself. Only nonconformity can save her, and finding her own voice is the only remedy for a bad case of stripes.

Who, What, When, and Why

★ What does Camilla Cream love to eat? Why doesn't she eat what she loves? Why is she not being honest with herself?

★ Why does Camilla try on forty-two outfits for the first day of school?

★ The TV news called Camilla "The Bizarre Case of the Incredible Changing Kid." What causes Camilla to change from stripes, to polka dots, to a pill bottle?

★ What cures her bad case of stripes?

READING TOGETHER

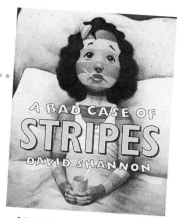

READ TOGETHER: GRADES K–2
READ ALONE: GRADES 2–3

 ## Look Closer

☆ Camilla doesn't eat lima beans because she wants to fit in with her friends who hate lima beans. What do you do to fit in?

☆ Have you ever tried on forty-two outfits for the first day of school? Why?

☆ Do you worry about what other people think of you?

Souvenir

"I knew the real you was in there somewhere."

What I Noticed

I wonder how important it is to me what other people think of me.

What did you notice?

 ## Quotes

"A man cannot be comfortable without his own approval."
—MARK TWAIN

 # Next

Check out these other titles:

Dandelion
BY DON FREEMAN

Elvira
BY MARGARET SHANNON

Ruby, The Copycat
BY PEGGY RATHMAN

Story of Ferdinand
BY MUNRO LEAF

Under the Cherry Tree
BY ALAN SAY

Weslandia
BY PAUL FLEISCHMAN

A Bargain for Frances

Russell Hoban

Doing the right thing, easily influenced, fairness, friendship, getting even, playing tricks on friends

Story Synopsis

Thelma has a way of outsmarting Frances, and one day she tricks Frances into buying her old plastic tea set. When Thelma states "no backsies," Frances comes up with a plan to teach her friend a lesson.

Who, What, When, and Why

★ Why does Frances's mother tell her to be careful when she plays with Thelma? Why does Frances need to be careful?
What would you think if your parents told you to be careful when playing with a friend?

★ Why does Frances buy Thelma's tea set when this is not the tea set she wants and she knows exactly what kind of tea set she wants to buy?
Are you easily influenced by others and talked out of what you think?

★ Are you suspicious when Thelma tells Frances there are no backsies once she buys the tea set?
Why is she trying to trick Frances?
Is Thelma a bad person?

★ What does Frances do to get even with Thelma? Do you think it was the right thing to do?
Is Frances a bad person?

READING TOGETHER

An I Can Read Book
LEVEL 2 Grades 1-3

A BARGAIN FOR FRANCES

by Russell Hoban
Pictures by Lillian Hoban

READ TOGETHER: GRADES K–1
READ ALONE: GRADES 1–3

 Souvenir

"'That is not a very nice trick to play on a friend,' said Thelma."

What I Noticed

I need to be careful not to be easily swayed.

What did you notice?

 **Quotes**

"The only way to have a friend is to be one."
—RALPH WALDO EMERSON

 Look Closer

☆ Frances tells Thelma that being careful is not as much fun as being friends. Do you agree?

☆ Do you think this will be the last time something like this happens between Frances and Thelma? How would you deal with a friend like Thelma?

☆ Frances decides to get even with Thelma by giving her a dose of her own medicine. Do you think it was fair for her to trick Thelma? Do two wrongs make a right?

☆ Who are you more like—Frances or Thelma? Or are you a little bit of both?

Next

Check out these other titles:

Frog and Toad
BY ARNOLD LOBEL

George and Martha
BY GEORGE MARSHALL

Houndsley and Catina
BY JAMES HOWE

Hunter's Best Friend at School
BY LAURA MALONE ELLIOTT

Rats on the Roof
BY GEORGE MARSHALL

Beatrice's Goat

Page McBrier

WORLD OF IDEAS

Helping someone help themselves, hopes and dreams, luck, making a difference, poverty

Story Synopsis

A story about how one small animal opened up a whole new world and made possible a young girl's dream of attending school in her small Ugandan village after her family is given an income-producing goat. Based on a true story about the work of Heifer Project International.

Who, What, When, and Why

★ Beatrice doesn't understand why a goat could turn out to be such a good gift but she agrees to help her mother get ready for it. What are some the things Beatrice does to get ready for the goat?

★ Beatrice thinks her family needs to buy a new shirt for Moses and a warm blanket. What does her mother decide needs to come before they buy all the things they need?
Why does she decide that school for Beatrice must come first?

★ Why does her mom call the goat a lucky gift? What kind of luck does Mugisa bring Beatrice and her family?
How does Mugisa improve Beatrice's community?

BY PAGE McBRIER · ILLUSTRATED BY LORI LOHSTOETER

Beatrice's Goat

with an afterword by
HILLARY RODHAM CLINTON

A NEW YORK TIMES BEST-SELLER

READ TOGETHER: GRADES 1–3
READ ALONE: GRADES 2–3

Look Closer

☆ What animal would you choose to give Beatrice's family? How could a horse, a pig, chickens, a dog, or a cat help Beatrice's family?
Would you choose to give them money?
Would money be a better gift?
How is Beatrice's education, a gift that will help her, help others?

☆ Beatrice has a dream. Do you have a dream? What is it?

☆ Can you accomplish your dream by yourself or do you need some help?
What do you need to make your dream happen—perseverance, patience, effort, imagination, luck?

Souvenir

"Good things take time."

What I Noticed

The story made me think about the kinds of gifts I get and the kinds of gifts I want to give.

What did you notice?

 **Quotes**

"Luck is a matter of preparation meeting opportunity."
—OPRAH WINFREY

Next

Check out these other titles:

Listen to the Wind
BY GREG MORTENSON

The Lost Horse
BY ED YOUNG

One Hen
BY KATIE SMITH MILWAY

Planting the Trees of Kenya
BY CLAIRE A. NIVOLA

Rag Coat
BY LAUREN A. MILLS

Bently and egg

William Joyce

Story Synopsis

Bently is an artist and a musician. One day he finds himself caring for his best friend's egg. With artistic flair he paints the dull, brown egg, making it beautiful. When an eager boy on an Easter egg hunt snatches the lovely egg, Bently finds himself on an adventure to rescue and safely return the egg to his friend.

Who, What, When, and Why

★ Bently and Kack Kack are best friends who take care of each other. Why does Kack Kack ask Bently to watch her egg? How does he feel about this?

★ Bently doesn't like the egg. He thinks it is too "bald and bare." What does he do to make the egg more to his liking?

★ The beautifully painted egg catches the attention of a young boy who takes it, thinking it is an Easter egg. Why does Bently think he has to save the egg?
What are some of the adventures Bently encounters in his efforts to save the egg?

★ Unfortunately Bently's beautiful decorations are washed clean during the rescue. Why does Bently comes to love the "bald and bare" egg? Is it because he rescued the egg and felt responsible for it?
Why does Kack Kack name her new son Ben?

BENTLY & egg

Story and Pictures by WILLIAM JOYCE

READ TOGETHER: GRADES PRE-K–2
READ ALONE: GRADES 1–3

Look Closer

☆ Bently uses big words such as *pandemonium, rapture, serenade, plummet, hors d' oeuvres, shimmering, valiantly.* Do you like big words? What big words do you like?

☆ Bently thought Kack Kack was his only friend until he discovered there were creatures out there "waiting" to become his friend. Who might be "waiting" to become your new friend?
Is it easy to make new friends? What makes it fun to make a new friend?

☆ On first impression Bently did not like the egg, but after he got to know the egg, he loved the egg. Is it better to get to know someone or something before you decide if you like or don't like it?

Souvenir

"Whenever he felt extremely happy he would burst into song."

What I Noticed

I loved Bently's paintings and poetry. My favorite painting was the one he did for the little girl who was sick.

What did you notice?

 Quotes

"*Friendship is the only cement that will ever hold the world together.*"
—WOODROW WILSON

Next

Check out these other titles:

An Extraordinary Egg
BY LEO LIONNI

Are You My Mother?
BY P. D. EASTMAN

Emma's Rug
BY ALLEN SAY

Fortunately
BY REMY CHARLIP

Horton Hatches the Egg
BY DR. SEUSS

The Talking Eggs
BY ROBERT D. SAN SOUCI

Courage

Bernard Waber

Story Synopsis

A story about the many faces of courage needed to stand up to an array of uncertainties and doubts. Courage is getting a new haircut, courage is going to bed without a flashlight, courage is a spelling bee ... courage is courage.

Who, What, When, and Why

★ Are pluck, daring, nerve, confidence, audacious, and spunk other words for courage?

★ Are cold feet, apprehension, anxiety, doubt, timidity, and being hesitant the opposite of courage?

★ Why does it take courage ...
   to be the new kid on the block and say hi?
   to be the first one to make up after an argument?
   to hold on to your dreams?
   to sometimes have to say good-bye?

★ Can anybody and everybody have courage?

READING TOGETHER

COURAGE
Bernard Waber

READ TOGETHER: GRADES K–2
READ ALONE: GRADES 1–3

 # Look Closer

☆ Can you go through life without courage?

☆ Does it take courage to try anything for the first time?

☆ Does courage always have to be daring, gallant, and bold?

☆ Can you be scared and courageous at the same time?

 ## Souvenir

"Courage is what we give to each other."

What I Noticed

The book made me see that I have more courage than I thought. Courage is courage, whatever kind.

What did you notice?

 ## Quotes

"Courage is rightly esteemed the first of human qualities because . . . it is the quality that guarantees all others."
—WINSTON CHURCHILL

 # Next

Check out these other titles:

Amos and Boris
BY WILLIAM STEIG

Feelings
BY ALIKI

The Little Yellow Leaf
BY CARIN BERGER

Owen
BY KEVIN HENKES

Rikki-Tikki-Tavi
BY RUDYARD KIPLING

Tillie and the Wall
BY LEO LIONNI

We're Going on a Bear Hunt
BY MICHAEL ROSEN

Elvira

Margaret Shannon

WORLD OF IDEAS

Courage, daring to be different, feeling appreciated, fitting in, individuality, teasing, resourcefulness

Story Synopsis

Elvira dislikes gobbling up princesses and fighting with the other dragons; she likes to dress up and make daisy chains. The other dragons tease and make fun of her, and in a fit of anger she leaves her home and joins the princesses.

Who, What, When, and Why

★ Elvira is different from the other dragons. What does she like to do?
What do the other little dragons like to do?
Why do the other little dragons tease her? How does this make Elvira feel?

★ What does Elvira do when her mother tells her she should just behave like a normal dragon? Where does Elvira go?
Why are the princesses at first not happy to see Elvira? How do their feelings change?
What do the princesses do to make Elvira feel "thrilled"?
Why don't Elvira's parents recognize her when they met her in the forest? How has she changed?
Why do the little dragons, who once teased Elvira, now want to be just like her?

READ TOGETHER: GRADES PRE-K–2
READ ALONE: GRADES 1–3

Souvenir

"'You want me to be like them?' This was too much."

 # Look Closer

☆ Why does Elvira's mother worry about her being different? Is she worried Elvira will have no friends and be lonely?
Do you ever feel like you don't fit in? How does that make you feel?
Do you like to be different? Does it take courage to be different?

☆ Elvira is teased by the other little dragons. Why do they tease her? Is it because she's different, do they not like her, are they jealous of her, or do they just not understand her?
Why do children tease other children? Is it fun to tease? Why?

What I Noticed

I was glad Elvira was able to breathe fire and prove to her dad that she was not a princess. I was worried he might eat her.

What did you notice?

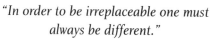 ## Quotes

"In order to be irreplaceable one must always be different."
—COCO CHANEL

 # Next

Check out these other titles:

A Color of His Own
BY LEO LIONNI

A Bad Case of Stripes
BY DAVID SHANNON

How to Be
BY LISA BROWN

In the Rain with Baby Duck
BY AMY HEST

Sneetches
BY DR. SEUSS

Stanley
BY SYD HOFF

The Story of Ferdinand
BY MUNRO LEAF

Enemy Pie

Derek Munson

WORLD OF IDEAS

Cleverness, conflicts, enemies, new friendships, open-mindedness, relationships

Story Synopsis

Hoping that the enemy pie, which his father makes, will help him get rid of his enemy, a little boy finds that instead it helps him make a new friend.

Who, What, When, and Why

★ Jeremy Ross ruined a perfect summer. What does he do that made him become "enemy #1"?
What is the dad's solution for how to deal with an enemy?
Why does the boy have to spend a day with his enemy in order for enemy pie to work? Why does he have to be nice to him?

★ The boy is scared to spend the day with his enemy and thinks it will be terrible. How does the day turn out? What do the boys do together?
What is the secret ingredient of the dad's enemy pie—butter, flour, sugar, and *nice?*

READ TOGETHER: GRADES K–2
READ ALONE: GRADES 2–3

 # Look Closer

☆ A tree house in your backyard, your brother or sister away at camp, and being on the best baseball team made for a perfect summer . . . What would make a perfect summer for you?

☆ Enemy pie tastes delicious and seems to work its magic. Could you make bully pie, class-know-it-all pie, or snob pie? What secret ingredient would you have to include in any of these pies?

☆ What makes Jeremy Ross an enemy? How does he turn out to be a friend? Have you ever had an enemy who turned out to be a friend?

Souvenir

"'Tell you how? I'll show you how!' he said."

What I Noticed

I was glad the dad did not put rocks, earthworms, and weeds into the enemy pie.

What did you notice?

Next

Check out these other titles:

Mean Soup
BY BETSY EVERITT

Feelings
BY ALIKI

King of the Playground
BY PHYLLIS REYNOLDS NAYLOR

Lovable Lyle
BY BERNARD WABER

 ## Quotes

"A thousand friends are few; one enemy is too many."
—RUSSIAN PROVERB

Farfallina and Marcel

Holly Keller

Butterflies and caterpillars, consideration, empathy, learning to be a good friend, respect, transformation, unlikely friendships

Story Synopsis

Farfallina, a caterpillar, and Marcel, a gosling, meet in a rain shower and become the best of friends. They play and respect each other as best friends do. One day Farfallina climbs a tree and never comes down. Marcel spends the winter waiting for his friend to return. When Farfallina does return, she is a butterfly and Marcel has grown from a gosling into a goose. The butterfly and the goose become "new friends' and realize each other's true identities.

Who, What, When, and Why

★ **Farfallina and Marcel meet one day, begin to play, and become friends. What do they like about each other?**
When they play hide-and-seek, how does Farfallina respect Marcel by hiding under a fern?
How does Marcel respect Farfallina by hiding close to her, behind the tree?

★ **What happens to Farfallina up in the tree? How does she change?**
How is Marcel able to recognize Farfallina after she changes from a caterpillar into a butterfly?

★ **How does Marcel change?**
How is Farfallina able to recognize Marcel after he changes from a gosling into a goose?

farfallina
& marcel

READ TOGETHER: GRADES PRE-K–2
READ ALONE: GRADES 1–3

 ## Souvenir

"'It's funny,' Marcel said, 'but I feel as though I've known you for a long time.'"

 # Look Closer

☆ When you play with certain friends, do you need to take into consideration how you play with that friend?

☆ If your best friend wore a costume, how would you know the person in the costume was your best friend—by their smile, by the way they treated you, by their laugh, by the way they played with you . . . ?

☆ Farfallina is an Italian word. Do you know what it means?*

What I Noticed

I loved the pictures of Farfallina riding on Marcel's back when she was a caterpillar and when she was a butterfly.

What did you notice?

 ## Quotes

"Friends are the sunshine of life."
—JOHN HAY

Next

Check out these other titles:

Bently and egg
BY WILLIAM JOYCE

First the Egg
BY LAURA VACCARO SEEGER

Hurry and the Monarch
BY ANTOINE FLATHARTA

Louie
BY ERZA JACK KEATS

Peach and Blue
BY SARAH KILBORNE

*Answer: *Farfallina* means "little butterfly" in Italian.

Frederick

Leo Lionni

WORLD OF IDEAS

Appreciating differences,
being yourself,
imagination,
power of words

Story Synopsis

Frederick was lost in his dreams while his family gathered nuts and seeds in preparation for winter. What they didn't know was that Fredrick was gathering images and words to help the mice during the long, dark days of cold.

Who, What, When, and Why

★ What are the mice doing to get ready for winter?

★ Why are the mice annoyed with Frederick? Do they understand his type of work?

★ What kind of work does Frederick do?

★ What good comes out of Frederick's work?

Frederick

Leo Lionni

READ TOGETHER: GRADES PRE-K–2
READ ALONE: GRADES 1–3

 # Look Closer

☆ Would you have found it difficult to understand and appreciate Frederick's type of work?

☆ Are there things you do that people might not appreciate? Do you have to understand something to appreciate it?

☆ Frederick was a dreamer and a poet. Do you know anyone who is a dreamer or a poet? Are you a dreamer? Are you a poet?

Souvenir

"I gather sun rays for the cold, dark winter days. I gather colors for winter is gray. I gather words for the winter days are long and many, and we'll run out of things to say."

What I Noticed

Frederick's red poppies, blue periwinkles, and his yellow wheat brought me sunshine.

What did you notice?

 Quotes

"Nobody can count himself an artist unless he carries a picture in his head before he paints it."
—CLAUDE MONET

 # Next

Check out these other titles:

The Bat-Poet
BY RANDALL JARRELL

Little Mouse's Painting
BY DIANE WOLKSTEIN

My Name Is Georgia
BY JEANETTE WINTER

Nutshell Library
BY MAURICE SENDAK

Puddle Pail
BY ELISA KLEVEN

Wabi Sabi
BY MARK REIBSTEIN

Grandfather's Journey

Allen Say

WORLD OF IDEAS

Curiosity, homesick, immigrant experience, restlessness

Story Synopsis

As a young man Allen Say's grandfather traveled from Japan to America, settling in California. He grew to love his new country, but missed his home in Japan. When he moved his family back to Japan he missed his home in California. He loved both countries.

Who, What, When, and Why

★ Grandfather leaves his home in Japan to see the world.
What kinds of clothes does he wear on his voyage to America?
What most impresses him—the Pacific Ocean, the deserts, the farm fields, the big buildings in the cities?
Of all the places he visits, what place does he like the best? Why?

★ Why does Grandfather return to Japan? Is he homesick?
When Grandfather is in California he misses Japan and when he is in Japan he misses California. Is he homesick for two places at the same time?

Grandfather's Journey

ALLEN SAY

READ TOGETHER: GRADES K–2
READ ALONE: GRADES 1–3

 Souvenir

"The funny thing is, the moment I am in one country, I am homesick for the other."

 # Look Closer

☆ Have you ever felt homesick—when you were away at camp, an overnight at a friends' house, on a trip, visiting a relative?
Do you feel homesick in your stomach, in your heart, or in your head?
Have you ever felt instantly "at home" in a new place, a place that resonated with you?

☆ What country are your grandparents from? Do they ever go back and visit their homeland? Do they miss the place they were born? Did they have to leave their homeland or did they leave voluntarily?
What do they do that reminds them of their homeland? Do they cook certain foods, celebrate different holidays, or speak a different language?

 ## What I Noticed

I couldn't decide which picture was my favorite but if I had to choose one, it would be the endless farm fields that reminded the grandfather of the ocean.

What did you notice?

 ## Quotes

"God gave us memory that we might have roses in December."

—SIR JAMES M. BARRIE

 # Next

Check out these other titles:

The Boy of the Three-Year Nap
BY DIANNE SNYDER

Castle on Hester Street
BY LINDA HELLER

The Cat Who Went to Heaven
BY ELIZABETH COATSWORTH

The Keeping Quilt
BY PATRICIA POLACCO

The Tale of the Mandarin Duck,
BY KATHERINE PATERSON

Watch the Stars Come Out
BY RIKI LEVINSON

Henrietta and the Golden Eggs

Hanna Johansen

WORLD OF IDEAS

Ambition, can-do attitude,
having a dream,
persistence,
self-confidence

Story Synopsis

Henrietta, a tiny hen, lives in an over-crowded, smelly chicken house where she dreams of learning to swim and sing and, most important, to lay a golden egg. The other 3,333 chickens laugh at her ambitions but that doesn't stop Henrietta from working on making her dreams come true.

Who, What, When, and Why

★ Why don't the 3,333 chickens like living in the chicken house?
What does Henrietta discover about the world outside the chicken house?

★ What words describe Henrietta—*ambitious, persistent, curious, a dreamer, an idealist, resolute, confident, unwavering*? What makes Henrietta think she can learn to sing, swim, and lay golden eggs?

★ What words describe the other chickens—*disapproving, unimaginative, boring, negative, not very confident, cynical*?

★ Every time Henrietta says she is going to learn something new, her fellow chickens say, "Don't bother trying." Why do they say that? Are they jealous, or are they worried Henrietta will be disappointed or frustrated if she fails.

★ Henrietta changes the lives of everyone in the henhouse forever. Does it matter that her first egg was not a golden egg, but a brown egg?
Do you think Henrietta was disappointed? Were you disappointed?

Hanna
Johansen

Henrietta
and the
Golden
Eggs

Pictures by
Käthi
Bhend

TRANSLATED BY
JOHN S BARRETT

READ TOGETHER: GRADES K–2
READ ALONE: GRADES 2–3

Souvenir

"'Don't even bother trying,' said the big chickens. 'Well, I'm going to try anyway,' said Henrietta."

What I Noticed

I hope I am more like Henrietta and not like the other chickens. I like her "can do" attitude.

What did you notice?

 Quotes

"Where there is a will, there is a way."
—PAULINE KAEL

 ## Look Closer

☆ Do you need a can-do attitude to make a dream happen? What do you need to have a can-do attitude—self-confidence, persistence, diligence, imagination, optimism, not afraid of failing?

☆ How easily are you influenced by what others think or say?
If someone told you, "Don't bother trying," would it stop you from trying?

☆ "Little" can sometimes be an advantage. Can you think of a situation when being little could be an advantage? Can you think of a situation when being little would be a disadvantage?

 ## Next

Check out these other titles:

Amos and Boris
BY WILLIAM STEIG

The Chicken-Chasing Queen of Lamar County
BY JANICE N. HARRINGTON

Minerva Louise and the Red Truck
BY JANET MORGAN STOEKE

The Golden Goose
BY DICK KING-SMITH

Henny Penny
BY JANE WATTENBERG

The Story of Jumping Mouse
BY JOHN STEPTOE

Tillie and the Wall
BY LEO LIONNI

Henry Hikes to Fitchburg

D. B. Johnson

WORLD OF IDEAS

Different approaches
to life, journeys,
living in harmony with nature,
winning and losing

Story Synopsis

Henry and his friend decide to go to Fitchburg. While his friend works hard to earn enough for train fare, Henry, a bear modeled on a young Henry David Thoreau, walks through the woods and fields with time to enjoy his surroundings. One walks and the other travels by train. Who gets to Fitchburg first?

Who, What, When, and Why

★ Henry's friend works to earn the fare so he can take the train to Fitchburg. What kinds of jobs does he do? How much money does he need for the train fare?

★ Henry decides to walk to Fitchburg. What does he do and see on his walk? How many miles does he walk? (Check out the road signs.).

★ Who gets to Fitchburg faster, the friend who takes the train or Henry who walks?
What is the fastest way to travel—walking or riding the train?
What makes Henry get to Fitchburg after his friend?

READ TOGETHER: GRADES PRE-K–2
READ ALONE: GRADES 1–3

Souvenir

"'Enjoy your walk,' he said. 'Enjoy your work,' he called back."

Look Closer

☆ Henry says walking is the fastest way to travel but his friend who takes the train arrives before him. Do you think Henry is disappointed that his friend arrives first?

Who do you think had more fun in getting to Fitchburg?

Who would you choose to travel to Fitchburg with, Henry or his friend?

Who would your mom or dad choose to travel to Fitchburg with?

☆ What is more important to Henry—getting to Fitchburg quickly or taking his time and enjoying the journey?

When you travel, do you consider the "getting there" as part of the journey or just a means to an end?

What I Noticed

Henry's friend had a pocketwatch (check out the pictures), but Henry didn't have a watch.

What did you notice?

 **Quotes**

"An early-morning walk is a blessing for the whole day."
—HENRY DAVID THOREAU

Next

Check out these other titles:

Aesop's Fables
BY CAROL WATSON

Henry David's House
BY HENRY THOREAU
AND STEVEN SCHNUR (EDITOR)

Henry David Thoreau
BY MILTON MELTZER

*Three Days on a
River in a Red Canoe*
BY VERA B. WILLIAMS

The Tortoise and the Hare
BY JANET STEVENS

Walking with Henry
BY THOMAS LOCKER

Hunter's Best Friend at School

Laura Malone Elliott

WORLD OF IDEAS

Clowning around, doing the right thing, friendship, mischief, peer pressure, setting a good example

Story Synopsis

Hunter and Stripe are best friends, and Stripe comes to school one day in a mischief-making mood. Stripe entices Hunter to go along with his clowning around, even though Hunter is not sure he should. Hunter has to figure out a way to get his best friend to be his best self.

Who, What, When, and Why

★ Stripe comes to school in a mischief-making mood. What does he do to make mischief?
Do you ever like to clown around? Who in your class likes to clown around?

★ Why does Hunter follow Stripe's urges to cut up his paper frog? How does he feel after he cuts up his paper frog?

★ What does Mr. Ringtail say to Hunter after he cuts up his frog? What could he have said?

★ Hunter's mom says you don't have to go along with your best friend. What else does she say about what it means to be a best friend?

★ What does Hunter do to help Stripe be his best self?

Hunter's Best Friend at School

By Laura Malone Elliott • Illustrations by Lynn Munsinger

READ TOGETHER: GRADES PRE-K–2
READ ALONE: GRADES 1–3

Souvenir

"Being a best friend doesn't mean always following along. Sometimes being a best friend means you have to help your friend be his best self."

What I Noticed

I never thought that helping someone be his best self was part of friendship.

What did you notice?

 Quotes

"Actions speak louder than words."
—AMERICAN PROVERB

Look Closer

☆ What makes Hunter like Stripe?
Is Stripe a bad friend for Hunter?

☆ Who is your best friend? Do you always go along with what he or she says?
Do you like your best friend to go along with what you say or do?

☆ Do you worry that your friends might not like you if you don't go along with their suggestions?
Is it hard not to go along with your friends, especially when it looks like fun?

☆ Are you more like Hunter or Stripe?
Or a little bit of both?

Next

Check out these other titles:

A Bargain for Frances
BY RUSSELL HOBAN

Cardboard Piano
BY LYNNE RAE PERKINS

Elvira
BY MARGARET SHANNON

Iris and Walter
BY ELISSA HADEN GUEST

Miss Bindergarten Has a Wild Day in Kindergarten
BY JOSEPH SLATE

Timothy's Tales from Hilltop School
BY ROSEMARY WELLS

It Could Always Be Worse

Margot Zemach

WORLD OF IDEAS

Appreciating what you have, attitude, complaining, humor, perspective, wisdom

Story Synopsis

If you think a hut is crowded with a wife, a mother, and six children, all quarreling and crying—try adding a few chickens, a rooster, a goose, a cow, and an old goat!

Who, What, When, and Why

★ A poor, unfortunate man goes to the rabbi to seek advice on how to improve his lot. He is poor, he has six children, and they live in a small hut, which is noisy and crowded. The rabbi advises the man to take his farm animals one by one into the hut to live with them. What happened? Did this help?

★ Then the rabbi advises the man to let *all* of the farm animals out of the hut. What happened? Did this help?

★ At the end of the story the poor, unfortunate man is back to where he started from, living with his large and noisy family in his small hut. Why does he say his hut is now "so quiet, so roomy, so peaceful, and such a pleasure"?

READ TOGETHER: GRADES PRE-K–2
READ ALONE: GRADES 1–3

Souvenir

"Rabbi, it couldn't be worse."

Look Closer

☆ Why does the unfortunate man listen to the rabbi even as the situation gets worse? Does he think the rabbi is a wise man?
Would you follow the rabbi's advice?

☆ Do you believe that it could always be worse?
How does changing your perspective change a situaton?

What I Noticed

The story made me think of what my buddy George always says: "If your head hurts, drop a rock on your toe, then your head won't hurt so much."

What did you notice?

Quotes

"Nobody tries to steal your troubles."
—YIDDISH FOLK SAYING

Next

Check out these other titles:

Could Be Worse!
BY JAMES STEVENSON

The Fortune-Tellers
BY LLOYD ALEXANDER

It Happened in Chelm
BY FLORENCE B. FREEDMAN

Martha Speaks
BY SUSAN MEDDAUGH

Ming Lo Loves the Mountain
BY ARNOLD LOBEL

Zlateh the Goat and Other Stories
BY ISAAC BASHEVIS SINGER

Julius, the Baby of the World

Kevin Henkes

WORLD OF IDEAS

Family dynamics, jealousy, loyalty, new sibling

Story Synopsis

Lilly's parents beam that "Julius is the Baby of the World," but Lilly, his sister, thinks he is disgusting. She can't understand why they make such a fuss over him, but when Lilly's cousin comes to visit, Lilly has a change of heart about Julius, the baby of the world.

Who, What, When, and Why

★ Before Julius is born Lilly gives him things, tells him secrets, and sings him lullabies. After Julius is born, how does Lilly treat him?
Why does Lilly think Julius is disgusting? Is she jealous of him, does he take up too much of her parents' time, does she just not like him?
Why does Lilly spend more time than usual in the uncooperative chair?
Why does Lilly run away seven times in one morning?

★ Lilly's parents tell Julius how beautiful he is and how much they love him. Why do they want Julius to be extraordinary and clever? Who do they want Julius to grow up to be like?

★ Why do Lilly's parents shower her with hugs and kisses and treats? Why doesn't this make her feel better?

★ Why does Lilly get annoyed when her cousin says Julius is disgusting? She has said the very same thing. What makes it okay for Lilly to speak ill of Julius but not anyone else?

JULIUS
THE BABY OF THE WORLD

KEVIN HENKES

READ TOGETHER: GRADES PRE-K–2
READ ALONE: GRADES 1–3

 Look Closer

☆ Is there an uncooperative chair in your house?

☆ Have you ever felt your parents loved a new baby (or an older or younger brother or sister) more than they loved you—even when they tell you how much they love you and shower you with treats and give you extra privileges?

Souvenir

"Before Julius was born, Lilly was the best big sister in the world."

What I Noticed

I never heard of anyone running away seven times in one morning.

What did you notice?

 **Quotes**

"Dear Me! What a troublesome business a family is."
—CHARLES KINGSLEY

Next

Check out these other titles:

I'll Fix Anthony
BY JUDITH VIORST

I'm a Big Brother and *I'm a Big Sister*
BY JOANNA COLE

Max's Bunny Business
BY ROSEMARY WELLS

On the Day You Were Born
BY DEBRA FRAISER

Russell and Elisa
BY JOHANNA HURWITZ

Sarah's Room
BY DORIS ORGEL

Ten Little Fingers and Ten Little Toes
BY MEM FOX

The Lost Horse

Ed Young

WORLD OF IDEAS

Changing
fortunes in life,
good fortune,
misfortune,
unexpected turnabouts

Story Synopsis

An ancient Chinese folktale about Sai, a man who owned a marvelous horse. When Sai lost his horse, his friends tried to console him, but he believed that things were not always as bad, or as good, as they might seem. A tale of how fortune can bring misfortune and misfortune can bring fortune.

Who, What, When, and Why

★ When Sai loses his horse, is he sad? Why not?
   When his horse returns with a mare, is he happy? Why not?
   When his son breaks his leg riding the mare, is Sai sad? Why not?

ED YOUNG

THE LOST HORSE

READ TOGETHER: GRADES K–2
READ ALONE: GRADES 1–3

 ## Souvenir

"Sai's son had learned from his father to trust in the ever-changing fortunes of life."

 # Look Closer

☆ Do you believe that things happen for the best?
Do you think you always know what's best?

☆ Have you ever thought something was terrible but it proved to be the exact opposite?
You wanted Teacher A but you got Teacher B. How did it work out?
You wanted to play on the Yellow Team but were chosen for the Green Team. How did it work out?
You wanted to be King Mazal in the play but you were chosen to be King Mazal's dog. How did it work out?

What I Noticed

I liked how Sai was able to see the cycle of good fortune, bad fortune, good fortune, bad fortune, good fortune . . .

What did you notice?

 ## Quotes

"A loss may turn out to be a gain."
—CHINESE PROVERB

 # Next

Check out these other titles:

Bea and Mr. Jones
BY AMY SCHWARTZ

Fortunately
BY REMY CHARLIP

Henrietta and the Golden Eggs
BY HANNA JOHANSEN

It Could Always Be Worse
BY MARGOT ZEMACH

Tikki Tikki Tembo
BY ARLENE MOSEL

Yeh-Shen: A Cinderella Story from China
BY AI-LING LOUIS

Many Moons

James Thurber

Story Synopsis

Princess Lenore wants the moon for a present and her father, the king, promises to fulfill her wish. The king implores the Lord High Chamberlain, the court wizard, and the court mathematician to get the moon for the princess. They all say it is impossible and it is only the court jester who consults the princess and is able to fulfill her one wish.

Who, What, When, and Why

★ The king asks his wisemen to get Princess Lenore the moon but they all proclaim it is impossible—nobody can get the moon.
What kind of things does the Lord High Chamberlain procure for the king? Why can't he get Princess Lenore the moon?
What kinds of magic does the royal wizard work for the king? Why can't he get Princess Lenore the moon?
What does the royal mathematician figure out for the king? Why can't he get Princess Lenore the moon?

★ Why is the court jester able to get Princess Lenore the moon? Is he smarter than the others, more clever, more thoughtful, wiser, or does he just use common sense?

★ Why don't the wisemen consult Princess Lenore and ask her exactly what she expects the moon to look like? Are the wisemen wise?

A CALDECOTT MEDAL WINNER

MANY MOONS

BY
JAMES THURBER
ILLUSTRATED BY
LOUIS SLOBODKIN

A Voyager/HBJ Book

READ TOGETHER: GRADES K–2
READ ALONE: GRADES 2–3

Souvenir

"One day Lenore fell ill of a surfeit of raspberry tarts and took to her bed."

 # Look Closer

☆ Princess Lenore asks for the moon. What would you ask for—a rainbow, a mountain, a river, a lake, an iceberg, a glacier, a volcano? Why?

☆ Samarkand, Zanzibar, Araby, Elfland are places mentioned in the story. Can you find them on a map?
Do black orchids, gold bugs, pink elephants, angels' feathers, eagles' tears, and the price of priceless exist?

☆ Do you think the moon is made of molten copper, green cheese, asbestos, or something else?
What is a blue moon? What does the expression "once in a blue moon" mean?

What I Noticed

I would like to be a clever person with a "surfeit of common sense."

What did you notice?

 ## Quotes

"It is not what you call us, but what we answer that matters."
—DJUKA PROVERB

 # Next

Check out these other titles:

Blue Moon Mountain
BY GERALDINE MCCAUGHREAN

Fireflies
BY JULIE BRINCKLOE

Lady Lollipop
BY DICK KING-SMITH

The Moon in My Room
BY URI SHULEVITZ

Night Wonders
BY JANE ANN PEDDICORD

Starry Messenger: Galileo Galilei
BY PETER SÍS

The Three Robbers
BY TOMI UNGERER

Mike Mulligan and His Steam Shovel

Virginia Lee Burton

Achievement, attitude, bragging, determination, effort, encouragement, pride, "why not?"

Story Synopsis

Mike Mulligan and his steam shovel Mary Anne made quite a team, but with progress and new machines, the two found themselves out of work. Modern shovels made them outdated but their determination and good work in digging Popperville's town hall proved their value.

Who, What, When, and Why

★ Mike Mulligan is very proud of his steam shovel Mary Anne, and he takes very good care of her. Why do the new gas, electric, and diesel shovels get all the jobs?
What do Mike Mulligan, Mary Anne, and "some others" accomplish?
Why do they work faster when people stop to watch them?

★ Why does Mike Mulligan say Mary Anne could dig as much in a day as a hundred men could dig in a week? Has she ever done that?
Did Henry B. Swap believe Mary Anne could dig as much in a day as a hundred men could dig in a week? Why does he give Mary Anne the job?
What do you think makes Mike Mulligan and Mary Anne successful at digging the new town hall in one day?

★ What is the solution to the dilemma of Mary Anne and Mike Mulligan forgetting to leave a way out? Who comes up with the solution? What do the people in Popperville think of the solution?
Do you think if you go to Popperville you will see Mike Mulligan and Mary Anne in the cellar of the town hall?

READ TOGETHER: GRADES PRE-K–2
READ ALONE: GRADES 1–3

Look Closer

☆ Why do people brag? Do you brag about something or someone you don't like? Do you have to be proud of something to boast about it?
Do you ever doubt a boast?

☆ Do you work faster and achieve more when someone is watching you? Why or why not?

☆ What do you think "why not" means? Does "why not" mean it's a good idea? Do you ever say "why not"?

Souvenir

"Everybody started talking at once, and everybody had a different idea, and everybody thought that his idea was the best."

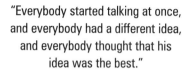

What I Noticed

I didn't like Henry B. Swap at the beginning of the story, but I changed my mind after I saw him sitting with Mike Mulligan and listening to his stories.

What did you notice?

Quotes

"It ain't braggin' if you can do it."
—DIZZY DEAN

Next

Check out these other titles:

Cars and Trucks and Things That Go
BY RICHARD SCARRY

Diggers and Dumpers
BY DK PUBLISHING

Henrietta and the Golden Eggs
BY HANNA JOHANSEN

The Little Engine That Could
BY WATTY PIPER

Seymour Simon's Book of Trucks
BY SEYMOUR SIMON

The Story About Ping
BY MARJORIE FLACK

Miss Rumphius

Barbara Cooney

Generosity, making a
difference, passion,
pursuing a dream

Story Synopsis

As a child, Alice Rumphius resolved that when she grew up she would go to faraway places, live by the sea in her old age, and do something to make the world more beautiful—and she does all those things, the last being the most difficult of all.

Who, What, When, and Why

★ **What does Alice want to do when she grows up?**
Her grandfather tells her she must do something to make the world more beautiful. What does he mean? Do you think it is a reasonable request?

★ **What does Miss Rumphius do to make the world more beautiful?**
What could you do to make the world more beautiful?

READ TOGETHER: GRADES K–2
READ ALONE: GRADES 1–3

 ## Look Closer

☆ Can you make the world more beautiful in small ways, in ways that everyone might not notice?

☆ When you are little, can you make the world more beautiful, or do you have to be an adult to make the world more beautiful?

☆ What would the world be like if nobody thought to make the world a better place (more beautiful)? Had you ever thought about making the world a more beautiful place before you read this story?

 ## Souvenir

"You must do something to make the world more beautiful . . . but I do not know yet what that can be."

 ## What I Noticed

I loved how Miss Rumphius traveled the world and had the patience to discover how she would carry out her grandfather's request to make the world more beautiful.

What did you notice?

 ## Next

Check out these other titles:

Angelo
BY DAVID MACAULAY

The Carrot Seed
BY RUTH KRAUSS

Johnny Appleseed
BY WILL MOSES

Tomás and the Library Lady
BY PAT MORA

What's This?
BY CAROLINE MOCKFORD

Wonder Bears
BY TAO NYEU

 ## Quotes

"Talk does not cook rice."
—CHINESE PROVERB

The Old Woman
Who Named Things

Cynthia Rylant

WORLD OF IDEAS

Acceptance,
independence,
loneliness,
luck, resilience

Story Synopsis

An old woman who has outlived all of her friends is reluctant to become too attached to the stray dog that visits her each day. When the dog disappears, she admits his place in her affections and after she finds him she gives him the name Lucky.

Who, What, When, and Why

★ **Who are Betsy, Fred, Roxanne, and Franklin?**
Why does the old woman name things? Why does this make her happy?

★ **Why does the puppy continue to come to the old womans house?**
Why doesn't the old woman want to name the puppy?
The old woman doesn't name the puppy. He doesn't belong to her so why is she sad when he no longer comes to her home?
Why does she name the dog Lucky? Why does the old woman think she is lucky?

READ TOGETHER: GRADES K–2
READ ALONE: GRADES 1–3

 # Look Closer

☆ What would you name your car, your favorite chair, your bed, your house, or a dog?

☆ The old woman says she is lucky because she has known so many friends in her life. What makes you feel lucky—your friends, family, talents, opportunities?

Souvenir

"Every morning she would get out of Roxanne, have a cup of cocoa in Fred, lock up Franklin, and drive to the post office in Betsy."

What I Noticed

I loved the old woman's shoes. She is wearing cowboy boots in almost every picture.

What did you notice?

Quotes

"Love makes the world go round."
—FRENCH PROVERB

Next

Check out these other titles:

Amos and Boris
BY WILLIAM STEIG

Farfallina and Marcel
BY HOLLY KELLER

Miss Rumphius
BY BARBARA COONEY

Peach and Blue
BY SARAH KILBORNE

Somebody Loves You, Mr. Hatch
BY EILEEN SPINELLI

Wilfrid Gordon McDonald Partridge
BY MEM FOX

Ruby the Copycat

Peggy Rathman

Coincidence, copying, fitting in, individuality, liking who you are

Story Synopsis

t's the first day of school for Ruby who insists on copying her classmate Angela, until her teacher helps her discover better ways to fit in by showing her how much fun it is to be herself.

Who, What, When, and Why

★ Do you think it is a coincidence that Ruby and Angela were both flower girls in their sisters' weddings?
Was it also a coincidence they both wore red bows in their hair, the same sweaters with daisies, and the same hand-painted T-shirts with matching sneakers?

★ Why did Angela run home and change into a black dress when, by coincidence, both she and Ruby had come to school that day in red-and-lavender-striped dresses?
What does Ruby discover she is good at? When Ruby discovers what she is good at, why does she stop copying Angela?

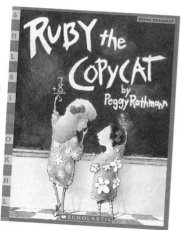

READ TOGETHER: GRADES PRE-K–2
READ ALONE: GRADES 1–3

Look Closer

☆ What is your first reaction when someone copies you?
Do you like when people copy you?
What do you like about people copying you?
What do you dislike about people copying you?
When does someone copying you become annoying?
Do you ever copy anyone? Why do people copy others?

☆ Ruby discovers she is good at hopping. What are you good at?

Souvenir

"You can be anything you want to be, but be Ruby first. I like Ruby."

What I Noticed

I was happy that Ruby disdcoverd what she was good at and that she and Angela became friends.

What did you notice?

  Quotes

"Imitation is the sincerest of flattery."
—CHARLES CALEB COLTON

Next

Check out these other titles:

Alexander and the Wind-Up Mouse
BY LEO LIONNI

A Bad Case of Stripes
BY DAVID SHANNON

Chrysanthemum
BY KEVIN HENKES

Lottie's New Friend
BY PETRA MATHERS

The Story of Ferdinand
BY MUNRO LEAF

You Look Ridiculous
BY BERNARD WABER

Widget
BY LYN ROSSITER MCFARLAND

Sam, Bangs and Moonshine

Evaline Ness

WORLD OF IDEAS

Consequences, exaggeration, gullible, lies, telling "stories," telling the truth

Story Synopsis

Sam is prone to telling tales of gross exaggeration and is warned repeatedly by her father not to tell "moonshine," as he refers to her tales and stories. An unintended consequence to one of her moonshine stories forces Sam to learn the difference between make-believe and real life.

Who, What, When, and Why

★ Sam has a reckless habit of lying. Is lying the same as telling "stories"?
Sam says her mother is a mermaid and she has a baby kangaroo at home. Why does she tell these "stories"? Are they lies? Or does Sam just have a vivid imagination?
What is the difference between "moonshine" and "real" talk?
Is "moonshine" the world Sam would like to live in?
Is "real" the world Sam lives in?

★ What does Sam's father mean when he says there is good "moonshine" and bad "moonshine"?
"Moonshine" is Sam telling Thomas that the baby kangaroo went to visit her mother, the mermaid, behind Blue Rock. Why does this "moonshine" spell trouble?

★ Thomas is gullible and believes every word Sam says. How does this get Thomas into trouble?

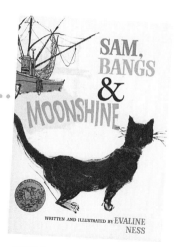

SAM, BANGS & MOONSHINE

WRITTEN AND ILLUSTRATED BY EVALINE NESS

READ TOGETHER: GRADES K–2
READ ALONE: GRADES 2–3

Look Closer

☆ Are you gullible?
Sam doesn't realize there could be serious consequences by telling "stories." Do you ever stop to think that making up "stories" could have serious consequences?
Do you always know when someone is making up a story?

Souvenir

"'There's good moonshine and bad moonshine,' he said. 'The important thing is to know the difference.'"

What I Noticed

I loved Sam's moonshine—especially when she says her mother is a mermaid—but I also realize how dangerous moonshine can be.

What did you notice?

Quotes

"Everybody, soon or late, sits down to a banquet of consequences."
—ROBERT LOUIS STEVENSON

Next

Check out these other titles:

And to Think That I Saw It on Mulberry Street
BY DR. SEUSS

Ernst
BY ELISA KLEVEN

Field Beyond the Outfield
BY MARK TEAGUE

Gooney Bird Green
BY LOIS LOWRY

Edwurd Fudwupper Fibbed Biz
BY BERKELEY BREATHED

John Patrick Norman McHennessy: The Boy Who Was Always Late
BY JOHN BURNINGHAM

Leon and Bob
BY SIMON JAMES

Scaredy Squirrel

Melanie Watt

WORLD OF IDEAS

Changing your routine, being well prepared, dangers, fear, predictability and unpredictability, self-awareness, worry

Story Synopsis

Scaredy Squirrel never leaves his nut tree. It's way too dangerous out there so he keeps to a precise, minute-by-minute daily schedule. One day his worst nightmare happens but he discovers to his astonishment that he is a flying squirrel. Eventually Scaredy Squirrel returns in triumph to his tree and from then on he adds a daily glide to his precise, minute-by-minute schedule.

Who, What, When, and Why

★ Scaredy Squirrel never leaves his tree and has no desire to risk venturing into the unknown. What is Scaredy Squirrel afraid of?
What does he do in his tree all day?
What does he have in his emergency kit?

★ There are advantages of never leaving the nut tree—great view, plenty of nuts, a safe place with none of the things he is afraid of. What are the disadvantages of never leaving the nut tree?

★ How does Scaredy Squirrel feel when he discovers he can fly? Why does flying make him forget about all of the things he was afraid of?

★ After his adventure, what is different in Scaredy Squirrel's routine?

READ TOGETHER: GRADES K–2
READ ALONE: GRADES 1–3

 ## Souvenir

"Finally Scaredy Squirrel realizes that nothing horrible is happening in the unknown today."

 # Look Closer

☆ What are you afraid of—the first day of school, camp, sleeping over at a friend's house, trying different foods, doing an activity without a friend? Have you ever been surprised that once you did any of those things, it wasn't so scary?

☆ What are some of the advantages of predictability? Do you like predictability? What are some of the disadvantages of predictability? Can predictability become boring?

☆ Would you be willing to give up a predictable routine to be surprised, astonished, and amazed?
If you gave up a predictable daily routine, might you discover something new about yourself?

 ## What I Noticed

I was glad Scaredy Squirrel's worst nightmare turned into a great adventure.

What did you notice?

 ## Quotes

"If you're never scared or embarrassed or hurt, it means you never take any chances."
—JULIA SOREL

 # Next

Check out these other titles:

Fortunately
BY REMY CHARLIP

Franklin in the Dark
BY PAULETTE BOURGEOIS

Some Things Are Scary
BY FLORENCE PARRY HEIDE

Switch on the Night
BY RAY BRADBURY

Tiny's Big Adventure
BY MARTIN WADDELL

Wemberly Worried
BY KEVIN HENKES

The Sneetches and Other Stories

Dr. Seuss

WORLD OF IDEAS

Being fooled, discrimination, envy, independent thinking, peer pressures, prejudice

Story Synopsis

A tale of the unfortunate Sneetches, bamboozled by one Sylvester McMonkey McBean ("the Fix-It-Up Chappie"), who shows them that pointless prejudice can be foolish as well as costly.

Who, What, When, and Why

★ Why do the Star-Bellied Sneetches think they are the best kind of Sneetch on the beach? Are they snobs, stuck-up, full of themselves, arrogant? Why do they discriminate against the Plain-Bellied Sneetches by not letting them play ball?

★ Why do the Plain-Bellied Sneetches think they are inferior to the Star-Bellied Sneetches? Do the Plain-Bellied Sneetches think having stars on their bellies would make them the best Sneetches on the beach?

★ What happens when the Sneetches keep going "in again, out again" in Sylvester McMonkey McBean's "Star-On and Star-Off" machine? Why do the Sneetches keep giving Sylvester McMonkey McBean their money?

★ At the end of the story, why are the Star-Bellied Sneetches friendly with the Plain-Bellied Sneetches? Did they know "which one was what one ... or what one was who?"

★ Sylvester McMonkey McBean says you can't teach a Sneetch. Is he right or wrong? How do the Sneetches get smart?

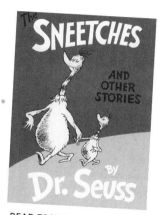

READ TOGETHER: GRADES K–2
READ ALONE: GRADES 2–3

 # Look Closer

☆ Do you know people who think they are better than others? Why do they think they are better?

☆ Does it take two sides for discrimination to work? Those who "dish it out" and those who accept it? Can someone make you feel inferior?

☆ Why is it easy to go along with a group? Why is it hard to stand up to a group?

Souvenir

 "[T]he Sneetches got really quite smart on that day,
The day they decided that Sneetches are Sneetches
And no kind of Sneetch is the best on the beach."

 ## What I Noticed

There will always be a Sylvester McMonkey McBean—someone ready and poised to promote and take advantage of discrimination.

What did you notice?

 ## Quotes

"No one can make you feel inferior without your consent."

—ELEANOR ROOSEVELT

Next

Check out these other titles:

The Lemming Condition
BY ALAN ARKIN

Nina Bonita
BY ELENA IRIBARREN

Nothing
BY JON AGEE

The Other Side
BY JACQUELINE WOODSON

Tico and the Golden Wings
BY LEO LIONNI

Two Eggs, Please
BY SARAH WEEKS

Tomás and the Library Lady

Pat Mora

WORLD OF IDEAS

Books as a window to the world, family, kindness, love of learning, making a difference, migrant family, storytelling

Story Synopsis

Tomás and his family, who are migrant workers, travel from state to state. In Iowa Tomás finds an entire world to explore in the books at the local public library. An added bonus—this is based on a true story.

Who, What, When, and Why

★ Why does Tomás's family live in Texas in the winter and in Iowa in the summer?

★ Tomás goes to the library to learn new stories that he can teach his Papa Grande who was the best storyteller in the family. Why is Tomás shy about going to the library?
What kinds of books does the librarian find for Tomás to read? What kinds of stories does Tomás get lost in?
The librarian lets Tomás check books out on her card. In exchange for her kindness what does Tomás teach the librarian?

★ What does Tomás do when he grows up? What building has his name on it today?

Look Closer

☆ What do you like about libraries—the story hour, the stacks of books and magazines you can check out, looking at the people who seem to be lost in their books?
What does it mean to get lost in a story? Would you like to be a librarian? What books would you recommend?

☆ Tomás likes being able to teach the librarian words in Spanish. What would you want to teach her?

☆ Who is the best storyteller in your family?
What kind of stories do they tell? Would you like to be the family storyteller?

Souvenir

"'What would you like to read about?' 'Tigers. Dinosaurs,' said Tomás."

What I Noticed

I loved that Tomás found a friend in the librarian. I liked that she let Tomás take out books on her card.

What did you notice?

 Quotes

"When I am reading a book, whether wise or silly, it seems to be alive and talking to me."
—JONATHAN SWIFT

Next

Check out these other titles:

A Day's Work
BY EVE BUNTING

Gathering the Sun
BY ALMA FLOR ADA

*Harvesting Hope:
The Story of Cesar Chavez*
BY KATHLEEN KRULL

The Library
BY SARAH STEWART

Library Lil
BY SUZANNE WILLIAMS

*Quiet! There's a Canary
in the Library*
BY DON FREEMAN

Unlovable

Dan Yaccarino

WORLD OF IDEAS

Being true to yourself, boasting, bullies, friendship, lying, sense of self, "shaky" self-esteem

Story Synopsis

Afred, a pug, is made to feel inferior by a cat, a parrot, and the other neighborhood dogs. When a new dog moves in next door, he helps Alfred realize he is fine just the way he is.

Who, What, When, and Why

★ Why do the cat, the parrot, and the goldfish make fun of Alfred? Why does Alfred think he is unlovable?

★ Why does Alfred boast and tell his new friend, Rex, he is a golden retriever? Does he think Rex won't like him if he knows he is a pug? Why is Alfred able to say he doesn't care what the others say? How does his friendship with Rex change the way Alfred feels about himself?

unLOVaBLe

Dan Yaccarino

READ TOGETHER: GRADES PRE-K–2
READ ALONE: GRADES 1–3

 Look Closer

☆ Why does Alfred believe the cat, the parrot, and the goldfish, who tell him he is unlovable? Does Alfred have a good sense of himself?
How does having self-esteem make it hard for people to tease you?

☆ At the end of the story Alfred is happy that Rex likes him just the way he is. If you change who you are, do you think people will like you?
How important is it to find friends that accept and like you for who you are?

Souvenir

"Who cared what the others said?"

What I Noticed

How could you not love Alfred, even though he snored and his legs were short!

What did you notice?

Quotes

"I am somebody. I am me, I like being me. And I need nobody to make me somebody."
—LOUIS L'AMOUR

Next

Check out these other titles:

Crictor
BY TOMI UNGERER

Dog and Bear
BY LAURA VACCARO SEEGER

Hooway for Wodney Wat
BY HELEN LESTER

Leo the Late Bloomer
BY ROBERT KRAUS

Pete and Pickles
BY BERKELEY BREATHED

Wanda's Monster

Eileen Spinelli

WORLD OF IDEAS

Empathy, fear, kindness, monsters, point of view, thoughtfulness

Story Synopsis

When Wanda fears that she has a monster in her closet, she takes her grandmother's advice and begins to look at things from the monster's point of view. With her newfound empathy, Wanda learns things she never knew about monsters.

Who, What, When, and Why

★ Except for Granny, everyone tells Wanda there isn't a monster in her closet. Granny not only says there is a monster but also explains to Wanda that monsters don't like to live in cold, dark closets.
Why do monsters hide from people?
What does Wanda do to make the monster more comfortable?
Why does Wanda give the monster her panda bear, a box of crayons, a cookie, and her favorite red scarf? Does Wanda come to like the monster?

★ Why does the monster have to leave?

Wanda's Monster

WRITTEN BY
Eileen Spinelli

ILLUSTRATED BY
Nancy Hayashi

READ TOGETHER: GRADES K–2
READ ALONE: GRADES 1–3

 Look Closer

☆ Do you think monsters are shy? Why else would they hide?
What storybook would you choose to read to a monster hiding in your closet?
What farewell gift would you give the monster in your closet?

☆ In addition to staying hidden and not staying in one closet for more than seventeen days and nights, what other rules do you think monsters might have?
What do you think monsters look like? Anything like Wanda's monster?

Souvenir

"'What does a monster care?' 'See? That's the kind of attitude monsters have to deal with.'"

What I Noticed

I liked how Granny knew about monsters. She understood their feelings.

What did you notice?

 Quotes

"Fear is created not by the world around us, but in the mind, by what we think is going to happen."
—ELIZABETH GAWAIN

Next

Check out these other titles:

Go Away, Big Green Monster!
BY ED EMBERLEY

The Gruffalo
BY JULIA DONALDSON

The Monster Who Ate Darkness
BY JOYCE DUNBAR

My Mama Says There Aren't Any Zombies, Ghosts, Vampires . . . or Things
BY JUDITH VIORST

There's a Monster Under My Bed
BY JAMES HOWE

There's a Nightmare in My Closet
BY MERCER MAYER

The Way to Start a Day

Byrd Baylor

WORLD OF IDEAS

Greeting a new day,
giving thanks,
rituals

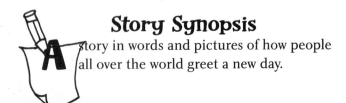

Story Synopsis

A story in words and pictures of how people all over the world greet a new day.

Who, What, When, and Why

★ In the Congo, people beat drums and in China people ring a thousand small gold bells—the morning needs to be sung to and a new day honored. How do the people in Peru, Mexico, Egypt, New Mexico, Japan, India, and Arizona honor a new day and greet the sun?

★ Flowers and sacred smoke are gifts some people give to the sun. What other gifts do people give?

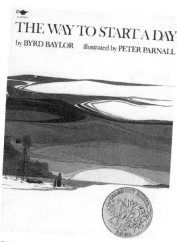

THE WAY TO START A DAY
by BYRD BAYLOR   illustrated by PETER PARNALL

READ TOGETHER: GRADES PRE-K–2
READ ALONE: GRADES 1–3

Look Closer

☆ The earth orbits the sun, the star at the center of the solar system. The sun gives light and warmth. Do you greet the sun? How would you like to greet the sun? What would the earth be like with no sun? Where does the sun rise where you live— in the front, in the back, on the side of your home?
When the sun comes up at your home, in what part of the world is the sun setting? How would you like to say good-bye to the sun at the end of the day?

☆ Can you find Peru, Mexico, the Congo, China, Egypt, New Mexico, Japan, India, and Arizona on a map? Can you find where you live on a map?

Souvenir

"When you feel the sun you'll feel the song too. Just sing it."

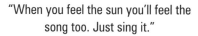

What I Noticed

I loved how in China people ring a thousand small gold bells to greet the day.

What did you notice?

Quotes

"Sunrise: day's great progenitor."
—EMILY DICKINSON

Next

Check out these other titles:

Backward Day
BY RUTH KRAUSS

Giving Thanks
BY JONATHAN LONDON

Head, Body, Legs
BY WON-LDY PAYE

Student Atlas 4th Edition
BY DK PUBLISHERS

The Sun
BY SEYMOUR SIMON

Sunshine
BY JAN ORMEROD

Whoever You Are
BY MEM FOX

When Sophie Gets Angry— Really, Really Angry ...

Molly Bang

WORLD OF IDEAS

Feelings, knowing yourself, managing anger, siblings

Story Synopsis

Sophie is playing with her stuffed gorilla, and she gets really mad when her sister grabs it and their mom says it is her sister's turn to play. Sophie becomes so angry that "she wants to smash the world to smithereens." Her anger takes many shapes as she tries to cool off and regain her composure.

Who, What, When, and Why

★ Why is Sophie angry? What does Sophie do when she gets angry?
Why does Sophie kick and scream, roar a red roar, explode like a volcano? Do these things make Sophie feel better?
Why does Sophie run until she can't run anymore and cry a little? Do these things make Sophie feel better?
Why does Sophie climb a tree and watch the water and waves? Do these things make Sophie feel better?

When Sophie Gets Angry— Really, Really Angry...

BY MOLLY BANG

READ TOGETHER: GRADES PRE-K–2
READ ALONE: GRADES 1–3

Souvenir

"The wide world comforts her."

 Look Closer

☆ What do you do when you get angry?
Do you shout, sulk, say angry things, say nothing?
Is it hard to tell someone you are angry?
Do you think it is possible to never be angry?
Can you ignore your anger until it goes away? Can you ignore a feeling?

☆ Is anger a "bad" feeling? Or is it "bad" just in the way you express your anger?
Do you think Sophie expressed and managed her anger in a good way?

☆ When you are angry, what makes you feel better—listening to music, eating something delicious, running and playing, telling someone why you are angry, giving yourself a "time-out"?

What I Noticed

When I get angry, being with my dog comforts me. When my mom gets angry, she doesn't like to talk, which makes my dad really angry. We all try not to get angry too often.

What did you notice?

 Quotes

"There is always a best way of doing everything."
—RALPH WALDO EMERSON

 **Next**

Check out these other titles:

How Are You Peeling?
BY SAXTON FREYMANN

Hurty Feelings
BY HELEN LESTER

Mean Soup
BY BETSY EVERITT

Sometimes You Get What You Want
BY LISA BROWN

Spinky Sulks
BY WILLIAM STEIG

Taking a Bath with a Dog and Other Things That Make Me Happy
BY SCOTT MENCHIN

Abel's Island

William Steig

WORLD OF IDEAS

Adventure, challenges,
confidence,
finding your passion,
resourcefulness,
self-reliance

Story Synopsis

Abel, a dignified and mannered mouse, seeks refuge in a cave with his wife, Amanda, during a terrible storm. Amanda's scarf is blown away and Abel leaves the safety of the cave to retrieve it. This valiant rescue attempt sends him out into the storm where he becomes lost and stranded on an island for a year. During this year of isolation Abel learns valuable lessons of survival and self-reliance.

Who, What, When, and Why

★ Abel impulsively runs after Amanda's scarf. What were the consequences of Abel's impulsive act?
Do you think it was a smart thing to do?

★ What keeps Abel from feeling too lonely? What keeps him busy?

★ What skills does Abel learn while on the island? Who are his "teachers"—nature, his friend Gower, himself?

★ At first Abel resents that he didn't choose this adventure. How do Abel's feelings about himself and his predicament change?

READING TOGETHER

Abel's Island

WILLIAM STEIG
A Caldecott Medal Winner and Newbery Honor Author

"The best book of the year."—*The New York Times*

READ TOGETHER: GRADES 2–4 +
READ ALONE: GRADES 3–5

Souvenir

"Having worked all day, seriously and well, he was warmed with a proper self-regard."

What I Noticed

I loved Abel's reflections about what mattered to him, what kind of mouse he was, and what his purpose was in life.

What did you notice?

Quotes

"Life is like a ten-speed bike. Most of us have gears we never use."
—CHARLES SCHULZ

 # Look Closer

☆ Abel says he has a "serious, real self" that is not part of his "show-off self." What is your real self?

☆ How does Abel grow into his name? How "able" would you be to survive such an adventure? How important are persistence, resourcefulness, confidence, and self-reliance in your being "able" to survive?

☆ Where do you learn to be self-reliant and resourceful? By having everything done for you or by doing things for yourself? Why does it feel good to do things for yourself?

☆ What situations have tested you? What is your attitude toward a challenging situation: "Why me?" and "It wasn't my fault," or "What can I learn from this situation?" and "How can I make the best of this?"

 # Next

Check out these other titles:

The Bat-Poet
BY RANDALL JARRELL

Ben and Me
BY ROBERT LAWSON

Perloo the Bold
BY AVI

Poppy
BY AVI

The Search for Delicious
BY NATALIE BABBITT

The Whipping Boy
BY SID FLEISCHMAN

Balto and the Great Race

Elizabeth Cody Kimmel

WORLD OF IDEAS

Adventure, Iditarod, intuition, overcoming obstacles, perseverance, sled dogs, teamwork, trust

Story Synopsis

A legendary story of a dog sled team's race to deliver medicine to a remote Alaskan village in 1925. Surviving countless obstacles and severe weather, Balto, the lead dog, and his musher, Gunnar Kaasen, deliver the needed medicine. The famous Iditarod race in Alaska is based on this heroic journey.

Who, What, When, and Why

★ Lead dogs must know how to respond to commands and keep the team moving. What other skills does a lead dog need?
Why do they use a relay of dogs and not one team of dogs to get the serum to Nome?

★ Balto isn't known for his speed and initially he wasn't chosen as the lead dog. What makes Kaasen change his mind and put Balto in charge?
What do you think is Balto's most important trait—his sense of smell, his tenacity, his intuition?

★ In addition to the 650-mile journey and the wildlife of Alaska, what are some of the other obstacles the mushers and dogs had to face?
What kinds of difficult decisions do the mushers have to make?
In what ways does Kaasen have to rely on the dogs?

READING TOGETHER

Balto and the Great Race

By Elizabeth Cody Kimmel
Illustrated by Nora Koerber

READ TOGETHER: GRADES 2–4+
READ ALONE: GRADES 3–5

Souvenir

"And most important of all, a lead dog must have intuition—a natural inner knowledge of what to do."

Look Closer

☆ What other kinds of situations can you think of where there is "no room for mistakes"?

☆ Would you be able to put your life in the "hands of a dog"? Could you have that much trust in a dog?

☆ A lead dog needs intuition—a natural inner knowledge of what to do. Are you born with intuition? How do you acquire it? How do you learn to trust your intuition?

Have you ever found yourself in a situation where you just "naturally" knew what to do, whether it was in sports or a situation with a friend?

What I Noticed

I had no idea sled dogs were so smart and intuitive. I love the idea that the famous Iditarod race retraces the route of Balto's journey.

What did you notice?

 Quotes

"Great works are performed not by strength, but by perseverance."
—SAMUEL JOHNSON

Next

Check out these other titles:

Dogteam
BY GARY PAULSEN

The Great Serum Race
BY DEBBIE S. MILLER

Mary on Horseback
BY ROSEMARY WELLS

Stone Fox
BY JOHN REYNOLDS GARDINER

Stickeen
BY JOHN MUIR
AND DONNELL RUBAY

Togo
BY ROBERT J. BLAKE

The Bat-Poet

Randall Jarrell

Curiosity,
difference, imagination,
misunderstanding,
open-mindedness,
persuasion, tolerance

Story Synopsis

Most bats sleep during the day and fly at night, but not the Bat-Poet. While the other bats slumber, the Bat-Poet stays awake and observes the world during the daylight. He begins to see the world differently from his nocturnal friends and, searching to find his own voice, he starts to write poetry.

Who, What, When, and Why

★ Why don't the bats want to stay awake during the day?
Why does the Bat-Poet try to persuade them to stay up and see the world by daylight?

★ Why does the Bat-Poet decide to share his poems with the mockingbird?
What disappoints him about the mockingbird's reaction to his poem?

★ Why does the chipmunk love the poem the Bat-Poet wrote for him?

★ Why is it easy for the Bat-Poet to write a poem about a mother bat and her baby?
What makes it difficult for the Bat-Poet to write a poem about the cardinal?

READING TOGETHER

THE BAT-POET
By Randall Jarrell
Pictures by Maurice Sendak

READ TOGETHER: GRADES 2–4+
READ ALONE: GRADES 3–5

Souvenir

"The trouble isn't making poems,
the trouble's finding somebody that
will listen to them."

What I Noticed

I liked how the Bat-Poet tried to
influence the other bats to see the
world from his point of view.

What did you notice?

 ## Quotes

"I don't know anything about art, but I know what I like."
—GELETT BURGES

 ## Look Closer

☆ The bats didn't want to try something
new. Is it hard to try something
new? Do you think it is fun or scary to try something new?

☆ Have you ever felt disappointed when
someone didn't appreciate or understand you?

☆ Can you write about something you
don't know well?
What makes it easier to write about something you know?

☆ Do you have to understand a poem to
like it?
Is it easier to like a poem you understand?

Next

Check out these other titles:

Abel's Island
BY WILLIAM STEIG

I'll Meet You at the Cucumbers
BY LILIAN MOORE

The Lemming Condition
BY ALAN ARKIN

Love That Dog
BY SHARON CREECH

Mouse Called Wolf
BY DICK KING-SMITH

The Mouse of Amherst
BY ELIZABETH SPIRES

Bird Boy

Elizabeth Starr Hill

Blame, bullies, disability, fear, playing tricks on friends, standing up for yourself, unintended consequences

Story Synopsis

Chang, who was born mute, lives on a houseboat with his parents on the Li River in China. With the use of trained cormorants, they earn their living catching fish. Chang wants more than anything to raise and train a baby cormorant. This hard-earned responsibility is tested when his friend Mei Mei's brother, Jinan, plays a trick on him.

Who, What, When, and Why

★ Jinan crashes his bicycle while chasing Chang, and he yells at Chang, "You got in my way!" Who is to blame for Jinan's bicycle accident?

★ Why does Chang try to get Jinan's bike out of the water? Does he feel sorry for Jinan or is there something else that motivates him?

★ While Chang is watching over the baby bird, Jinan offers Chang a chance to ride his bike. Why does Chang trust Jinan and accept his offer? Is Jinan just being nice?

★ Why does Chang refuse to let Jinan on his houseboat when Jinan asks him if he wants to play cards? Would you have accepted Jinan's offer to play cards? Would you have accepted his "I'm sorry"?

Bird Boy
ELIZABETH STARR HILL
Pictures by LESLEY LIU

A fascinating glimpse into a different world. —*Riverbank Review*

READ TOGETHER: GRADES 2–4
READ ALONE: GRADES 3–4+

Souvenir

"The little bird has spirit. It would try hard. And Chang had found that trying made all the difference."

 ## Look Closer

☆ How do you become a bully? Are people born bullies?

Are bullies happy people? Can you ever trust a bully?

Are bullies people who just don't know how to have or be a friend?

☆ Jinan tells Chang he didn't mean to hurt the chick; it was only a joke. When someone says "it was only a joke," what do they mean?

Do jokes have a way of getting out of hand with unintended consequences?

☆ Does "I didn't mean it" change a situation? Does "I'm sorry" change a situation?

 ## What I Noticed

I found it interesting that Chang, who couldn't talk, had Mei Mei as a friend but Jinan, who could talk, didn't know how to be a friend.

What did you notice?

 Quotes

"*Courage is resistance to fear, mastery of fear— not absence of fear.*"

—MARK TWAIN

Next

Check out these other titles:

Crow Boy
BY TARO YASHIMA

The Dragonling
BY JACKIE FRENCH KOLLER

The Hundred Dresses
BY ELEANOR ESTES

Kami and the Yaks
BY ANDREA STENN STRYER

The Year of Miss Agnes
BY KIRKPATRICK HILL

Blackberries in the Dark

Mavis Jukes

WORLD OF IDEAS

Change,
creating new traditions,
grandparents,
memories,
sadness

Story Synopsis

Every summer Austin stays with his grand-parents at their farm. After his grandfather dies, nine-year-old Austin visits his grand-mother and is worried how they will spend their time. This was the summer his grandfather was going to teach him to fly-fish. With an unexpected outing, Austin and his grandmother begin to create some of their own traditions.

Who, What, When, and Why

★ Why does Austin's grandmother tell him to go and pick the blackberries by himself? Why doesn't she go with him? Why does she change her mind? Why do they continue to fish and eat blackberries in the dark?
Eating blackberries in the dark was a family tradition. What is different this time?
How do their "new ways of being together" help them get closer?

★ Why does the grandmother give Austin her antique doll and his grandfather's fishing knife?

READ TOGETHER: GRADES 3–4
READ ALONE: GRADES 3–4+

 Look Closer

☆ What are some traditions you share with your family? Do you have a favorite tradition? Where did this tradition come from?
When you have a family of your own, which traditions will you keep?

☆ Is there something that has been in your family for a long time and handed down from generation to generation?

☆ What do you do with your grandmother? What do you do with your grandfather? Have you ever thought about changing what you do with each of them?

Souvenir

"'It's good luck to throw back the first fish of the season,' Grandpa said."

What I Noticed

I was glad the grandmother changed her mind and went fishing with Austin.

What did you notice?

Next

Check out these other titles:

Because of Winn-Dixie
BY KATE DICAMILLO

Missing May
BY CYNTHIA RYLANT

Ola's Wake
BY B. J. STONE

The Raft
BY JIM LAMARCHE

Sun and Spoon
BY KEVIN HENKES

 **Quotes**

"We do not remember days, we remember moments."
—CESARE PAVESE

Donavan's Word Jar

Monalisa DeGross

**Collecting,
coming up with your
own solutions, generosity,
making a difference**

Story Synopsis

t seemed like everyone in Donavan's class collected something, so when a word on a cereal box catches his fancy, Donavan starts to collect words. He finds interesting and new words everywhere and his collection grows. When Donavan's word jar fills up, he finds a unique way to give his words away with surprising results.

Who, What, When, and Why

★ **Why does Donavan start collecting words? What do his friends collect?**
What do you collect? What do your friends collect?

★ **Why is it difficult for Donavan to give away his words?**
Why does he become generous and decide to give his words away?

★ **At the end of the story, why does Donavan's grandmother call him a "wordgatherer"?**
What other names might he be called—a word wizard, a wordsmith, a master of words?

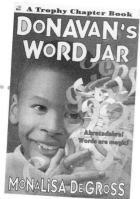

READ TOGETHER: GRADES 2–3+
READ ALONE: GRADES 3–4+

 ## Souvenir

"'Perseverance,' he called out. 'That's just the word I need. Some days I get so tired I can hardly make it. I'm going to try just a little harder to keep going,' he said, tucking the word in his shirt pocket."

What I Noticed

I never asked myself how words make me feel, and I never asked myself how my words make other people feel.

What did you notice?

 ## Quotes

"Generosity lies less in giving much than in giving at the right moment."
—JEAN DE LA BRUYÈRE

 # Look Closer

☆ Big words like *profound* made Donavan feel smart and little words like *cuddle* warmed his heart. Do certain words make you feel a certain way?
Do you have a favorite word?
Can you name a happy word, a magic word, a silly word, a get-well word?

☆ Donavan needs a solution for what to do with his word collection, and he doesn't like anybody's suggestions. Do you easily take suggestions from others, or do you like to find your own solutions?
When is it good to take other people's suggestions?
When is it good to find your own solutions?

☆ Are you being generous when you give somebody something you don't want?
Are you being generous when you give somebody something you have a lot of?

 # Next

Check out these other titles:

Blackberries in the Dark
BY MAVIS JUKES

The Boy Who Loved Words
BY RONI SCHOTTER

Frindle
BY ANDREW CLEMENTS

Miss Alaineus
BY DEBRA FRASIER

The Silver Balloon
BY SUSAN BONNERS

The Dragonling

Jackie French Koller

WORLD OF IDEAS

Courage, dragons, empathy, fear, heroes, peer pressure, preconceived ideas, standing up for your beliefs

Story Synopsis

Darek couldn't wait to be old enough to hunt and kill a dragon with his father and brother and the men in his village. The men return from a successful hunt with the body of an impressive Great Blue (one of the largest and fiercest of dragons). Darek sneaks out that night to see the slain dragon and finds a baby dragon safe and sound in the dead mother's pouch. Even though he was raised to hate dragons, Darek risks death and the anger of his people by trying to return the baby dragon to the Valley of the Dragons.

Who, What, When, and Why

★ Why in the beginning does Darek want to kill a dragon? Why does Darek's mother think hunting dragons is not necessary to prove you are a man? What other ways are there to prove you are a man?

★ What does Darek know about dragons before he meets Zantor? What are his preconceived ideas about dragons? Does anyone in his village know much about dragons?

★ What does Clep mean when he tells Darek that he was just lucky and what Darek did took courage? What is the difference between luck and courage? What takes more courage—Darek returning Zantor or Darek standing up to his father?
Who is the hero of the story—Clep, Darek, the moms of the village, or Zantor?

Ready-for-Chapters
The **Dragonling**

Can a boy and a dragon be friends?
Jackie French Koller

READ TOGETHER: GRADES 2–4
READ ALONE: GRADES 3–4+

Look Closer

☆ Where do we learn to fear the things we fear? Are fears based on preconceived ideas?

☆ Is it difficult not to be influenced by what others do and think?
What makes it hard to go against the majority?
Do you ever outgrow peer pressure?
Are adults immune from peer pressure?

☆ Darek's mother says that proving yourself as a man means doing your work with pride, caring for others, and thinking your own thoughts. Which of these would be the most important to you? Which would be the most difficult to do?

Souvenir

"Knowing what to do and doing it, however, were two different matters."

What I Noticed

The story made me realize why it is hard to stand up for your beliefs.

What did you notice?

Quotes

"It takes courage to grow up and become who you really are."

—E. E. CUMMINGS

Next

Check out these other titles:

The Dragon's Boy
BY JANE YOLEN

The Enchanted Forrest Chronicles
BY PATRICIA WREDE

The Enormous Egg
BY OLIVER BUTTERWORTH

My Father's Dragon
BY RUTH STILES GANNETT

The Reluctant Dragon
BY KENNETH GRAHAME

The Terrible Troll-Bird
BY INGRI D'AULAIRE

The Gold-Threaded Dress
Carolyn Marsden

WORLD OF IDEAS

Bullies, consequences,
doing the right thing,
lying, peer pressure,
popularity,
pride in your heritage

Story Synopsis

When Oy and her Thai American family move to a new neighborhood, her third-grade classmates tease and exclude her because she is different. She wants nothing more than to fit in and be popular with the girls. Her beautiful, ceremonial gold-threaded Thai dress holds the key to popularity, but also disaster.

Who, What, When, and Why

★ Who gets invited to join Liliandra's club?
Why is Oy not included?
Why does Oy want to join Liliandra's club?
What does Oy have to do to get into Liliandra's club?

★ Why does Frankie tease Oy? Is he being mean or is he trying to be friendly?
Is it always easy to recognize a gesture of friendship?

★ Why does Oy think Mere and Kun Pa don't understand her feelings?
What causes Oy to realize her parents do understand? How do they show her they understand?

CAROLYN MARSDEN

The Gold-Threaded Dress

What would you give up in order to fit in?

READ TOGETHER: GRADES 2–4
READ ALONE: GRADES 3–5

 Look Closer

☆ Who is an American?
Do you have to be born in America to be American?

☆ Do you have a Liliandra in your grade, the person who sets the rules the rest follow?
Why do people follow these self-appointed leaders?

☆ What is worse, you knowing you did something wrong or others knowing you did something wrong?

Souvenir

"'Remember, little daughter,' her mother says, 'the children are interested in this dress not because it makes them look the same, but because it makes them look different.'"

What I Noticed

I wonder how tempted I would be to do something a popular kid asked me to do just so I would fit in.

What did you notice?

Next

Check out these other titles:

The Hundred Dresses
BY ELEANOR ESTES

In the Year of the Boar and Jackie Robinson
BY BETTE BAO LORD

Jake Drake, Class Clown
BY ANDREW CLEMENTS

Seesaw Girl
BY LINDA SUE PARK

The Year of the Dog
BY GRACE LIN

 Quotes

"To forget one's ancestors is to be a brook without a source, a tree without root."
—CHINESE PROVERB

A Horn for Louis

Eric Kimmel

WORLD OF IDEAS

Aspirations, charity, friendship, jazz, Louis Armstrong, poverty, pride, shame, tenacity

Story Synopsis

This is the story of Louis Armstrong as a young boy living in New Orleans' Brick Row at the turn of the twentieth century. Life was not easy, but his relationship with a Russian immigrant family helped him get his first "real" horn and showed him that everyone needs help and can offer help as well.

Who, What, When, and Why

★ What is Louis's dream when he's seven years old? Do you have a dream?

★ Why doesn't Louis get to keep the money he earns at the Karnofskys' junkyard for himself?

★ Why do the Karnofskys want to give Louis a horn? Why does Louis tell the Karnofskys that he cannot accept the horn as a present?

★ Mr. Karnofsky tells Louis that when they came to America they needed help—everybody needs help sometimes. Why does Louis change his attitude about accepting the horn?

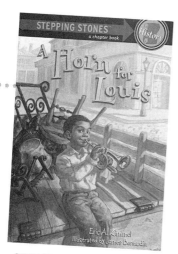

READ TOGETHER: GRADES 2–4
READ ALONE: GRADES 3–4+

Souvenir

"Never give up. Keep on trying.
You never know what you can
do until you try."

What I Noticed

I like the idea that if someone helps
you, then someday you will be able to
help someone else.

What did you notice?

 Quotes

*"Dreams come true; without that possibility, nature
would not invite us to have them."*

—JOHN UPDIKE

 Look Closer

☆ Pop tells Louis that everyone needs help
sometimes, the hard part is knowing how to
do it right. What does doing it "right" mean?

☆ Do you agree with Mr. Karnofsky who tells
Louis that you don't solve your problems by
running away?
Is there a problem you have wanted to run away
from?
What happens if you ignore a problem? Does
the problem just go away?

☆ Does music change your mood? Can music
make you happy, sad, reflective, mellow, or
energetic?
What kind of music do you like?
What kind of music does your mom or dad like?
Do you have a favorite instrument?

Next

Check out these other titles:

A Gift for Mama
BY ESTHER HAUTZIG

Before John Was a Jazz Giant
BY CAROLE BOSTON WEATHERFORD

Jazz
BY WALTER DEAN MYERS

*The Most Beautiful Place
in the World*
BY ANN CAMERON

Handel, Who Knew What He Liked
BY M. T. ANDERSON

This Jazz Man
BY KAREN EHRHARDT

The Hundred Dresses

Eleanor Estes

Complicity, courage, empathy, friendship, making amends, popularity, regret, teasing, thoughtlessness

Story Synopsis

Wanda Petronski, a Polish immigrant, is the new girl at school, and every day she wears the same faded blue dress. One day she tells Peggy, the most popular girl at school, and her best friend, Maddie, that in her closet she has a hundred dresses. Peggy just can't help but tease Wanda about these "unseen" dresses, and Maddie is unable to stand up and put a stop to the relentless teasing.

Who, What, When, and Why

★ Why does Wanda tell the girls she has a hundred dresses?

★ Why does Maddie go along with Peggy, who asks Wanda every day how many dresses she has? Maddie says teasing Wanda just sort of happened; there was nothing anyone could do about it. Do you agree with her?

★ Who do you think is more to blame: Peggy, who hadn't thought they were being mean, or Maddie, who didn't like the teasing but stood by silently?

★ After she learns that Wanda has moved, why does Maddie come to the conclusion that she will never stand by and say nothing again?

READ TOGETHER: GRADES 2–4
READ ALONE: GRADES 3–4+

Souvenir

"She had done just as much as Peggy to make life miserable for Wanda by simply standing by and saying nothing."

What I Noticed

I hope Maddie can keep her promise not to make anybody else so unhappy again.

What did you notice?

 Quotes

"The reward for conformity was that everyone liked you except yourself."
—RITA MAE BROWN

Look Closer

☆ **What makes Peggy popular? Who are the popular kids in your class?**
Who decides who is popular? How important is it to be popular?
Who would you want for a friend, Peggy, Maddie, or Wanda?

☆ **Maddie says she knew she would never have the courage to tell Peggy to stop teasing Wanda. Why is it difficult to speak up in these situations?**
Are you responsible to speak up when someone is doing something that you know is wrong?

☆ **Is it easy to hurt someone's feelings out of thoughtlessness?**
Does it matter whether it is deliberate or merely thoughtlessness that causes the hurt feelings?

☆ **Does saying "I'm sorry" make everything all right?**
Do you owe anyone an "I'm sorry"?

Next

Check out these other titles:

Because of Winn-Dixie
BY KATE DICAMILLO

The Family Under the Bridge
BY NATALIE SAVAGE CARLSON

The Girl with 500 Middle Names
BY MARGARET PETERSON HADDIX

The Gold-Threaded Dress
BY CAROLYN MARSDEN

Poppy
BY AVI

Jake Drake, Know-It-All

Andrew Clements

Story Synopsis

Jake Drake really wants to win the fourth-grade science fair prize, a brand-new computer. Jake refuses to work with his best friend, Willie, because he doesn't want to share the prize. He works day and night to win, competing with the class know-it-alls and finds that working alone and working all the time wasn't that much fun.

Who, What, When, and Why

★ Jake says there is nothing worse than a know-it-all. What makes Marsha and Kevin know-it-alls? What bothers Jake about them?
Is there a know-it-all in your class?
Did Jake care more about beating Kevin and less about doing a great project?
Did Pete care more about doing a great project and less about winning the prize?
What is Pete's advantage to have his hobby be his science fair project?
Why does Jake know Pete will be the winner? Why does interest and enjoyment matter so much?

★ Why does Jake change his mind and ask Willie to be his science fair partner?
What becomes more important to Jake—enjoying working as a team, winning, or beating Kevin?

★ How do Jake and Willie feel about winning second place?

Jake Drake
KNOW-IT-ALL
Can Jake come up with a winning
science fair project?

Andrew Clements
THE AUTHOR OF FRINDLE

READ TOGETHER: GRADES 2–4
READ ALONE: GRADES 3–4+

Souvenir

"It was like they thought school was a TV game show. If you get the right answer first, you win the big prize."

 Look Closer

☆ **Are you someone who says "I know it" almost automatically?**
Can you learn anything new when you say you already "know" it?

☆ **What are some of the benefits of working as a team?**
What are some of the benefits of working alone?
Which do you prefer? Why?

☆ **What happens when wanting to win becomes "I have to win"?**
What drives what you do—competition, fun, passion, wanting to be the best?

☆ **How do you feel when others turn in projects that are clearly not their own?**
Do you think they had fun doing the project?

What I Noticed

I am going to try to stop automatically saying, "I know it" all the time. I might even learn something new!

What did you notice?

 **Quotes**

"Pleasure in the job puts perfection in the work."
—ARISTOTLE

Next

Check out these other titles:

Gorky Rises
BY WILLIAM STEIG

The Great Brain
BY JOHN D. FITZGERALD

A Magic Crystal?
BY LOUIS SACHAR

Owen Foote, Soccer Star
BY STEPHANIE GREENE

Three Terrible Trins
BY DICK KING-SMITH

The King's Equal

Katherine Paterson

WORLD OF IDEAS

Common sense, greed, intelligence, kindness, pride, selfish, vanity, self-sufficiency

Story Synopsis

A dying king tells his spoiled son he cannot be king until he finds a princess that is his equal. The prince feels he is the smartest, most beautiful, and richest prince and has a difficult time meeting his equal. It is not until he meets Rosamund that he realizes the true definition of beauty, intelligence, and richness.

Who, What, When, and Why

★ The king tells Raphael he will not wear the crown until he marries a woman who is his equal. What qualities does the king say his future wife must possess?
Why does Raphael say this is a curse and not a blessing?

★ Rosamund is not schooled by scholars. What makes her intelligent?
She does not have jewels or land. What makes her wealthy?
She is not the best looking. What makes her beautiful?

★ Rosamund tells Raphael he must go live in the mountains for a year before she will consider marrying him. At the end of his year in the mountains, Raphael is still handsome, intelligent, and wealthy. What is different?
What does Raphael learn from the wolf in the mountains?

★ Why do Rosamund and Raphael return to the mountains every year?

READING TOGETHER

A Trophy Chapter Book

THE KING'S EQUAL

KATHERINE PATERSON

READ TOGETHER: GRADES 1–3
READ ALONE: GRADES 2–3+

 ## Look Closer

☆ You can be wealthy, intelligent, and beautiful and still be a nice person. What makes Raphael so obnoxious? How would adding humility, grace, and manners to the mix of wealth, intelligence, and beauty make a difference?

☆ Why do you think Rosamund is kind to the wolf? Does she expect a reward? What is your motivation for being kind to others? Do you think it is the right thing to do? Do you want people to think well of you? Do you expect to be rewarded for your kindness?

☆ Who would you like to live with, the wolf in the mountains or Rosamund and Raphael in the castle?

Souvenir

"A man who has friends is truly rich."

What I Noticed

I would never want to be incapable of taking care of myself like the prince was when he first went to live in the mountains with the goats.

What did you notice?

 ## Quotes

"Liberated women need liberated men."
—ARTHUR DOBRIN

Next

Check out these other titles:

The Fool of the World and the Flying Ship
BY ARTHUR RANSOME

Lady Lollipop
BY DICK KING-SMITH

Rapunzel
BY THE BROTHERS GRIMM
AND PAUL O. ZELINSKY

Sleeping Ugly
BY JANE YOLEN

The Whipping Boy
BY SID FLEISCHMAN

Lady Lollipop

Dick King-Smith

Being respectful, being spoiled, cleverness, learning new ways, manners, tantrums, unlikely friendships

Story Synopsis

Princess Penelope is spoiled "quite a bit" by her mother, the queen, and spoiled "rotten" by her father, the king. For her birthday, she demands a pig as her present. Princess Penelope learns some valuable lessons about manners and friendship as she observes Johnny Skinner train her new pig, Lollipop. The quick-witted Johnny and the smart pig are royally rewarded after they reform a spoiled princess.

Who, What, When, and Why

★ What makes Princess Penelope a "pain in the neck"?
Do people like her? Does she have many friends?

★ Why do you think her parents offer her so many choices for a birthday present?
Does her repeated response "I wanna pig" sound like a tantrum?
Is there a difference between a tantrum and wanting to have your own way?

★ Johnny Skinner says the princess is spoiled, "but in a way it is not her fault." Why isn't it entirely her fault? Whose fault is it?

★ Who is Johnny Skinner training, Lollipop or the princess?
Penelope wants Lollipop to listen to her. What advice does Johnny Skinner give her?

★ Who has changed the most at the end of the story—Lollipop, the princess, the king, or the queen?

Dick King-Smith

LADY LOLLIPOP

illustrated by Jill Barton

READ TOGETHER: GRADES 2–4
READ ALONE: GRADES 3–4+

Souvenir

"She needs to be taught to think more about other people and less about herself."

Look Closer

☆ How does a person become spoiled? Are people born spoiled?
Why do some parents spoil their children?
Are spoiled people enjoyable to be with?
How does a spoiled person act?

☆ The king says Penelope has a will of her own. What does it mean to have a will of your own?
Is having a will of your own the same as being opinioned, stubborn, wanting your own way, or knowing your own mind?
When is it good to have a will of your own?
Can you be too strong willed?

☆ Is "just this once" ever just this once?

☆ Would you want the princess for a friend? How long would that friendship last?
Do you know anyone like the princess?

What I Noticed

I admired Johnny Skinner's patience in teaching the royal family new ways.

What did you notice?

 Quotes

"Attitude is a little thing that makes a big difference."
—WINSTON CHURCHILL

Next

Check out these other titles:

Do Unto Otters
BY LAURIE KELLER

Manners
BY ALIKI

Manners Can Be Fun
BY MUNRO LEAF

Many Moons
BY JAMES THURBER

Pierre: A Cautionary Tale
BY MAURICE SENDAK

The Whipping Boy
BY SID FLEISCHMAN

Love That Dog

Sharon Creech

WORLD OF IDEAS

Confidence, dogs, finding your voice, first impressions, love of words, poetry, school assignments

Story Synopsis

Jack was convinced he did not like poetry and didn't see the value of his poetry assignments. With the help of his teacher, eight wonderful poets, and his favorite poet, Walter Dean Myers, Jack not only learns to enjoy poetry but also is inspired to write his own poetry. He realizes he is a poet.

Who, What, When, and Why

★ Why doesn't Jack like poetry? Does he think he is not good at it? Is he frustrated that the poems don't make any sense? Does he think poetry is only for girls?
Why doesn't he want the teacher to put his poems up for all to see?

★ Jack doesn't understand the wheelbarrow poem and thinks Robert Frost had too much time on his hands. Why does he like the poems by Miss Valerie Worth? Is it just because they are short and not intimidating?
Do her poems change his mind about what poetry can be?

★ The poem "Love That Boy" sparks Jack's enthusiasm. How does this poem help Jack make his story of his yellow dog into the poem "Love That Dog"?

SHARON CREECH
WINNER OF THE NEWBERY MEDAL FOR *WALK TWO MOONS*

LOVE
THAT
DOG

a novel

READ TOGETHER: GRADES 2–4
READ ALONE: GRADES 3–5+

Souvenir

"I don't want to because boys don't write poetry. Girls do."

What I Noticed

Love That Dog made me realize I can write poetry.

What did you notice?

 **Quotes**

"A poem is the best words in the best order."
—SAMUEL TAYLOR COLERIDGE

 Look Closer

☆ Why don't some people like poetry? Do you think you have to be smart to like or understand poetry?
Did you know that in the Inuit language "to make poetry" is the same word as "to breathe"?

☆ Do you think poetry is difficult and demanding? Can you write a poem about anything—chairs, pigs, pies, tractors, shoes, kites, brooms, eggs, soap bubbles?

☆ Jack says that Robert Frost's poetry was just "making pictures with words." What kinds of pictures can you make with words?

☆ If poetry is only for girls, as Jack thought, why are there so many famous male poets?

Next

Check out these other titles:

A Kick in the Head
BY PAUL B. JANECZKO

The Bat-Poet
BY RANDALL JARRELL

Dog Heaven
BY CYNTHIA RYLANT

Knock at a Star
BY X. J. KENNEDY

The Mouse of Amherst
BY ELIZABETH SPIRES

Sad Underwear
BY JUDITH VIORST

Someone I Like
EDITED BY JUDITH NICHOLLS

The Magic Paintbrush

Laurence Yep

WORLD OF IDEAS

Attitude, consequences, death, greed, hope, magic, memories, wishes

Story Synopsis

After Steve's parents die, he goes to live with his grandfather and his "uncle" Fong in San Francisco's Chinatown. Steve has a difficult time adjusting and doesn't understand his grandfather's stern and disapproving ways. Life changes after his grandfather gives Steve a paintbrush. This magic paintbrush transports Steve, his grandfather, and Uncle Fong from their drab apartment to a world of adventures.

Who, What, When, and Why

★ Why does Steve find it difficult to live with his grandfather and Uncle Fong?
Why is Steve's grandfather stern? Does he not like Steve?
Is he annoyed that Steve is now living with him?

★ What do Uncle Fong and Grandfather wish for? Do they get what they wish for?
What does Steve wish for? Does his wish come true?

★ What did Mr. Pang wish for? Why do you think the magic began to work against him?
Could it be that he was greedy and asked for too much?

★ What does Mr. Blue mean when he says magic cannot be tamed, it is like nature?
Why do you have to be careful with magic? Can you ever control magic?

READ TOGETHER: GRADES 2–4
READ ALONE: GRADES 3–5

Souvenir

"His grandfather really did care. He just didn't talk about it. He showed it by his actions."

Look Closer

☆ If you had to put your "whole life in a box," what things would you choose and why?

☆ Steve's grandfather says the past is past and you can't spend the rest of your life missing someone or something. Do you think it's possible to stop missing someone or something you loved?

☆ What do you need to be happy? Do you have what you need to be happy?
What would you paint with a magic paintbrush? What would you wish for?

☆ What are some of your favorite stories about magic?
In these stories, does magic always have a cost?

What I Noticed

At the end of the story I loved that Steve saw his tiny and cramped room in a new light, and I realized that a person's attitude is very important.

What did you notice?

Quotes

"We don't see things as they are; we see them as we are."
—THE TALMUD

Next

Check out these other titles:

Bright Shadow
BY AVI

The Castle in the Attic
BY ELIZABETH WINTHROP

Half Magic
BY EDWARD EAGER

The Lost Flower Children
BY JANET TAYLOR LISLE

The Story of the Treasure Seekers
BY EDITH NESBIT

The Mary Celeste:
An Unsolved Mystery from History
Jane Yolen and Heidi Elisabet Stemple

Adventure, curiosity, curses, pirates, unsolved mystery, yellow journalism

Story Synopsis

In 1872, the *Mary Celeste* sailed out of New York City, and three weeks later, Captain Morehouse and his crew found it abandoned, deserted with no captain, no crew. What happened? Was it pirates, mutiny, or illness? It remains a mystery.

Who, What, When, and Why

★ What do Captain Morehouse and his crew find when they board the *Mary Celeste*?
In addition to the ship being deserted, what else did they find?

★ Why do they think that the *Mary Celeste* might have been set upon by pirates?
What is wrong with this theory?

★ What is wrong with the theory that the crew became drunk and killed the captain and his family?

★ What motive could Captain Morehouse and his crew have for doing away with the crew and bringing in the empty *Mary Celeste* for salvage?

READING TOGETHER

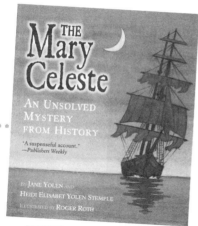

READ TOGETHER: GRADES 2–4
READ ALONE: GRADES 3–4+

Souvenir

"He says I was born curious, which is just what a detective needs to be."

What I Noticed

The story made me realize that I can't assume that everything I read is accurate.

What did you notice?

 ## Quotes

"I wanted to know the name of every stone and flower and insect and bird and beast . . . but there was no one to tell me."

—GEORGE WASHINGTON CARVER

 # Look Closer

☆ What would be fun about being a detective?

☆ What is your theory about what happened to the *Mary Celeste*?

☆ Do you believe in curses? What is the difference between a curse and just plain bad luck? What do people mean when they say, "That house is cursed"?
How is that different from saying, "That house just has bad luck"?

☆ Yellow journalism is when a newspaper makes up half-truths to thrill readers. Do you believe everything you read in a newspaper or on the Internet?
Do you think it is important to read more than one article from different sources to get at the truth?
Is it important to know what special interests lie behind a story?

Next

Check out these other titles:

The Giant Rat of Sumatra
BY SID FLEISCHMAN

The Great Ships
BY PATRICK O'BRIEN

Jack Plank Tells Tales
BY NATALIE BABBITT

Nellie Bly: A Name to Be Reckoned With
BY STEPHEN KRENSKY

Miss Alaineus

Debra Frasier

WORLD OF IDEAS

Blame,
embarrassment,
mistakes,
wordplay

Story Synopsis

Sage is absent from school one day and calls her friend Starr to get the spelling words for the week. While writing down the list, Sage misunderstands one of the vocabulary words. This "miss understanding" becomes a catastrophe and moves into a tragedy, which turns into a disaster and ends as a triumph.

Who, What, When, and Why

Answer these questions:

★ Sage misses the spelling test because of Forest. Is Forest:
(a) a thicket of trees (b) a berry bush (c) a boy sneezing and coughing all over Sage's desk

★ Sage calls Starr to get the list of vocabulary words. Is Starr:
(a) something you wish on (b) a luminous celestial object (c) a very smart girl who listens perfectly on Vocabulary Day

★ Which definition doesn't fit the word?
(a) *humbled*: aware of shortcomings, arrogant, modest, meek (b) *devastate*: create, waste, ravage (c) *ruined*: destroyed, preserved (d) *finished*: debut, brought to an end (e) *red*: the color of envy, the color of embarrassment

★ Extra credit: Choose a letter of the alphabet and write a sentence using four words (not three words) that start with that letter. For extra extra credit, choose the letter X.

★ Have fun!

READING TOGETHER

READ TOGETHER: GRADES 2–4
READ ALONE: GRADES 3–4+

Souvenir

"Not smiled—grinned: to draw back the lips and bare the teeth as in a very wide smile—and the entire class burst into one huge giggling, laughing, falling-down mass of kids."

What I Noticed

I waved and whistled and wished the book would never end.

What did you notice?

Look Closer

☆ Have you ever made a mistake that left you humbled, devastated, ruined, ravaged, or the color red?
Do you believe there is "gold in every mistake"? What does this mean?

☆ Do you have a "Miss Alaineus drawer"? What's in it?
Have you ever made a Miss Stake?
Do you like Miss Sterious things?

☆ If you had a vocabulary parade, what word would you choose?
What would your costume look like?

Next

Check out these other titles:

Chickerella
BY MARY JANE AUCH

Judy Moody
BY MEGAN MCDONALD

The Phantom Tollbooth
BY NORTON JUSTER

The Pig in the Spigot
BY RICHARD WILBUR

Scooter
BY VERA B. WILLIAMS

 Quotes

"Second tries aren't for losers, just another chance to win."
—RABBI JUDAH DARDIK

The Mouse of Amherst

Elizabeth Spires

WORLD OF IDEAS

Courage, curiosity,
confidence,
finding your calling,
inspiration,
love of words,
perseverance,
unlikely friendship

Story Synopsis

Emmaline, who considers herself a "mouse of little purpose," lives in the same house as the famous poet Emily Dickinson. Emmaline can't believe how Emily Dickinson's poetry accurately describes her feelings. She begins a correspondence with the poet that leads to a wonderful friendship.

Who, What, When, and Why

★ In addition to chasing the cat away, what does Emily do to show her friendship to Emmaline? What does Emmaline do to show Emily her friendship?

★ Why doesn't Mr. Higginson like Emily's poetry? Does he not understand her poetry?

★ Emmaline is conflicted over leaving the Dickinson home. What are her reasons for wanting to stay with Emily? What makes her decision to leave difficult?
How does Emily's poem about the sea give Emmaline the courage to know she has to leave?

READ TOGETHER: GRADES 2–4
READ ALONE: GRADES 3–5

Souvenir

"The words spoke to me. These were my feelings exactly, but ones I had always kept hidden for fear the world would think me a sentimental fool."

 Look Closer

☆ Emmaline says she always travels lightly but packs her dictionary. If you were moving to a new home, what would you pack? What book would you bring with you?

☆ Do you have to understand everything in a poem to like it? What is your favorite poem? (If your child doesn't have one, help him or her find one!)

☆ Would you continue to write poetry, draw a picture, or do anything if you knew it was never going to be appreciated? What is more important, your appreciation or the appreciation of another?

☆ Are you like Emmaline who asks herself, "Who am I?" and "Why am I here, where am I going?"

What I Noticed

I loved Emmaline's courage, her confidence, and her adventurous spirit. I wanted this story to be true!

What did you notice?

Next

Check out these other titles:

The Bat-Poet
BY RANDALL JARRELL

Ben and Me
BY ROBERT LAWSON

Emily
BY MICHAEL BEDARD

Love That Dog
BY SHARON CREECH

My Letter to the World
BY EMILY DICKINSON

A River of Words
BY JEN BRYANT

 **Quotes**

"To be an artist, one must ... never shirk from the truth as he understands it, never withdraw from life."
—DIEGO RIVERA

Mr. Popper's Penguins

Richard Atwater

Challenges, consequences, doing the right thing, dreams, loneliness, thinking of others, willingness to be different

Story Synopsis

Mr. Popper is a house painter, husband, and father with a burning desire to know and study everything about the North and South Poles. One day, to his surprise, Admiral Drake from the North Pole sends him a baby penguin. Little does Mr. Popper realize how one delightful penguin, along with eleven others, would change his life forever.

Who, What, When, and Why

★ What words describe Mr. Popper—*eccentric, creative, curious, thoughtful, adventurous?* Would you like to be like Mr. Popper? Why or why not?

★ What are some of the things Mr. Popper does to make sure his penguins are comfortable and happy living in his home?

★ Mr. Popper has a difficult time deciding what will be best for the penguins.
Why does he refuse Mr. Klein's offer for the penguins to go to Hollywood?
Why does he decide to give the penguins to Admiral Drake?

READING TOGETHER

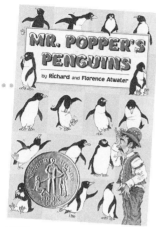

READ TOGETHER: GRADES 2–4
READ ALONE: GRADES 3–5

 ## Souvenir

"The birds have done so much for me that I have to do what is best for them."

 # Look Closer

☆ Mr. Popper is a dreamer and he is different from other people. How willing are you to be different? Are you a dreamer? Do you have a dream?

☆ Have you ever made a decision that you knew was the "right" decision for someone else, but not necessarily a decision that made you happy?
Do "right" decisions always make you feel good?

☆ Mrs. Popper doesn't tell Mr. Popper what he should do with the penguins; she lets him come to his own decision. Would you find it difficult to let someone make up his or her own mind and not give your opinion?

 ## What I Noticed

I loved that Mr. Popper was a dreamer, always dreaming of faraway countries and reading about famous adventurers.

What did you notice?

 Quotes

"Whatever you can do, or dream you can do, begin it. Boldness has genius and power in it."
—JOHANN WOLFGANG VON GOETHE

 # Next

Check out these other titles:

Babe: The Gallant Pig
BY DICK KING-SMITH

The Emperor Lays an Egg
BY BRENDA Z. GUIBERSON

My Season with Penguins
BY SOPHIE WEBB

Penguins
BY SEYMOUR SIMON

Tacky
BY HELEN LESTER

365 Penguins
BY JEAN-LUC FROMENTAL

Mysterious Miss Slade

Dick King-Smith

WORLD OF IDEAS

Compassion,
first impressions,
getting involved,
independent thinking,
loneliness,
unlikely friendships

Story Synopsis

Everyone thinks Miss Slade, who lives by herself with no electricity, no plumbing, and her six dogs, six cats, and various other animals, is a witch. When a new family moves into a cottage up the hill from Miss Slade, they befriend her and soon discover what lies behind the mysterious Miss Slade.

Who, What, When, and Why

★ What are the villagers' first impressions of Miss Slade? Why do they think she is a witch?
Miss Slade rides a donkey to get her groceries, wears a patch over one eye, lives with no electricity and plumbing, and her clothes are old and ratty. Other than the way she dresses and the way she lives, what do they really know about her?

★ Why do Patsy and Jim like Miss Slade? Why did they like to visit her? Why aren't they afraid of her like the other children?
What is the initial reaction of Jim and Patsy's parents to Miss Slade? Why does their reaction change?

★ Why did Miss Slade choose to live alone?
Why does Miss Slade decide to change her ways?

DICK KING-SMITH
AUTHOR OF BABE: THE GALLANT PIG

Mysterious Miss Slade

ILLUSTRATED BY ANN KRONHEIMER

READ TOGETHER: GRADES 2–4
READ ALONE: GRADES 3–5

Souvenir

"I'm not too old to learn a lesson."

Look Closer

☆ Do you trust first impressions? What makes first impressions so important and also so unreliable?
What impression would people get upon first meeting you?

☆ How do you get to know someone—by their reputation, their appearance, the opinions of others?
Can you know someone without knowing their "story"?

☆ How would your parents react to you having a friend like Miss Slade?
How would you react to your parents having a friend like Miss Slade?
Do you know anybody like Miss Slade?

What I Noticed

This story is a nice reminder that everyone has a story and that you can't really know someone without knowing their story.

What did you notice?

 ## Quotes

"Don't judge a book by its cover."
—ENGLISH PROVERB

Next

Check out these other titles:

Dominic
BY WILLIAM STEIG

The Dragonling
BY JACKIE FRENCH KOLLER

The Hundred Dresses
BY ELEANOR ESTES

Mrs. Piggle-Wiggle
BY BETTY MACDONALD

The Storm
BY CYNTHIA RYLANT

Nellie Bly:
A Name to Be Reckoned With
Stephen Krensky

WORLD OF IDEAS

Adventure, determination, journalism, nonconformity, persistence, resourcefulness, sticking up for yourself

Story Synopsis

In 1864, there were few opportunities for women to work, especially as serious news reporters. Nellie was determined to write and to write about serious subjects. Reporting was the heart and soul of Nellie Bly's life and her assignments ranged from a seventy-two-day race around the world to life inside a mental institution to the most important labor strike in history.

Who, What, When, and Why

★ What words describe Nellie Bly—*free-spirited, risk taker, determined, passionate, courageous, maverick, nonconformist?*
Why does Nellie insist on writing important stories of the day? What kinds of stories does Nellie write?
What makes her a good reporter?

★ What do you think is the most difficult story for her to write—her trip to Mexico, living inside the insane asylum, her trip around in the world, or the Pullman strike?
Which story would you choose to write about? Why?

★ When Nellie Bly covers the Pullman strike, she goes with firm ideas against the strikers. What does she discover and how does she report it?
Why are the other newspapers unwilling to criticize Pullman?

MILESTONE BOOKS

Nellie Bly
A Name to Be Reckoned With
by Stephen Krensky • Illustrated by Rebecca Guay

READ TOGETHER: GRADES 2–4
READ ALONE: GRADES 3–4+

Look Closer

☆ What would you take on a trip around the world?
Could you pack and get ready to leave with one day's notice?

☆ Is it a reporter's job to write her opinions, or the facts as she observes them? What makes it difficult to just write the facts?
How can you tell if someone is writing the facts or their opinions? How would you be able to discern a writer's bias?

☆ Do you trust everything you read—whether it is on the Internet, in a newspaper, or in a magazine?
Can you get the complete story from reading one source?

Souvenir

"Write up things as you find them, good or bad; give praise or blame as you think best; and all the truth all the time."

What I Noticed

I was impressed with Nellie Bly's integrity as a reporter. She wrote what she saw and not what she thought.

What did you notice?

Quotes

"Tell me what you pay attention to, and I will tell you who you are."
—JOSE ORTEGA Y GASSETT

Next

Check out these other titles:

The Daring Nellie Bly
BY BONNIE CHRISTENSEN

The Landry News
BY ANDREW CLEMENTS

*The Mary Celeste:
An Unsolved Mystery from History*
BY JANE YOLEN AND
HEIDI ELISABET STEMPLE

Mary on Horseback
BY ROSEMARY WELLS

*You Want Women to Vote,
Lizzie Stanton?*
BY JEAN FRITZ

No Flying in the House

Betty Brock

WORLD OF IDEAS

Choices, consequences, following your heart, love, magic, promises, secrets

Story Synopsis

Annabel Tippens, who does not have parents to look after her, has a tiny white dog named Gloria, who is no ordinary dog. Gloria can talk and perform the most unbelievable tricks. Mrs. Vancourt, a very proper lady who does not have a place for children in her orderly house, gives Annabel a home because she loves Gloria's tricks. In her new home Annabel finds out from the wicked cat, Belinda, that she is no ordinary girl—she is half fairy!

Who, What, When, and Why

★ Why does Mrs. Vancourt's son, Tommy, run away?
What does he bury in the garden before he runs away?

★ How does Annabel find out she is "part fairy"?
What does Belinda ask Annabel to do to prove she is a fairy?
Can you pass the test?
Why does Belinda think Annabel will love being a fairy?
Why doesn't Gloria want Annabel to find out she is half fairy?

★ Gloria loves Annabel and wants her to be a mortal, and Belinda thinks being a fairy is wonderful because fairies can fly. What promise did Gloria make to Princess Felicia, Annabel's mother? Why was this promise so important?
What will happen if Annabel chooses to be a fairy?
What will happen if Annabel chooses to be a mortal?
Why does she decide to be a mortal? What wins out, love or flying?

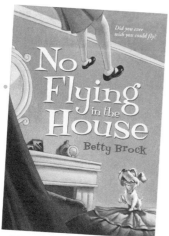

READ TOGETHER: GRADES 2–4
READ ALONE: GRADES 3–5

Souvenir

"Questions were going off inside
Annabel's head like popcorn."

What I Noticed

I was glad Annabel chose love over
the ability to fly.

What did you notice?

Look Closer

☆ Would the idea of being a fairy appeal
to you? Why or why not?
What would you love about being a fairy?
If you were Annabel, what choice would
you have made?

☆ Do you "listen to your heart"?
Is it sometimes hard to "hear" what your
heart is telling you?
What are the consequences of not following your heart?

☆ Do you believe, once a secret is shared,
that it can still be a secret?

Next

Check out these other titles:

Bright Shadow
BY AVI

The Lost Flower Children
BY JANET TAYLOR LISLE

The Magic Paintbrush
BY LAURENCE YEP

The Secret Garden
BY FRANCES HODGSON BURNETT

The Witch Family
BY ELEANOR ESTES

Quotes

*"If your head tells you one thing and your heart tells you another, before you do any-
thing, you should first decide whether you have a better head or a better heart."*
—MARILYN VOS SAVANT

One Small Dog

Johanna Hurwitz

WORLD OF IDEAS

Choices, divorce,
disappointment,
excuses, nagging,
responsibility,
running away

Story Synopsis

Curtis is in the fourth grade when his parents get divorced. Against her better judgment, his mom gives in and buys him a puppy. Curtis, unaware of the responsibilities of owning and training a puppy, gives excuse after excuse about the puppy's chewing and biting. After one too many excuses, Curtis realizes he needs to face the hard facts of owning a pet.

Who, What, When, and Why

★ Why does Curtis want a dog so badly? Do you think his mom gives in to his request too easily?
Why does she give in? Is she tired of Curtis's nagging?
Is it realistic for Curtis to promise his mom that she won't have to do anything for their new dog, Sammy?

★ Curtis has an answer for all of Sammy's mischief. Do you think they are reasonable explanations or excuses?
What mischief does Sammy do?
Why does Curtis wear his old sneakers?

★ Sammy snaps at Curtis's mom, Mitch, and finally at Curtis. The mom tells Curtis, "dogs that bite can't be pets," so they can't keep Sammy. Do you agree with her decision?
Why does Curtis run away?
Why doesn't his plan to run away work?

READING TOGETHER

One Small Dog

Johanna Hurwitz
Illustrated by Diane deGroat

READ TOGETHER: GRADES 2–4
READ ALONE: GRADES 3–4+

Souvenir

"But you know, that's how life is: happy and sad."

Look Closer

☆ **What is the difference between an explanation and an excuse?**
Why do people make excuses? Are they reluctant or unwilling to face the facts?

☆ **Does doing the "right thing" always make you feel good?**
Can you think of a situation when you did the right thing and it made you feel good?
Can you think of a situation when you did the right thing and it didn't feel so good?

☆ **Curtis wrote a story about Sammy. Does writing help you understand a situation? If yes, how? If no, why not?**
How would the story be told if the mom was telling the story?

☆ **Do you agree with the dog trainer who says that love is not enough to have a dog?**

What I Noticed

The story made me realize that doing the right thing does not always feel good.

What did you notice?

Quotes

"The girl who can't dance says the band can't play."
—YIDDISH PROVERB

Next

Check out these other titles:

Five True Dog Stories
BY MARGARET DAVIDSON

Fred Stays with Me
BY NANCY COFFLET

Not My Dog
BY COLBY F. RODOWSKY

The Real Thief
BY WILLIAM STEIG

Stone Fox
BY JOHN REYNOLDS GARDINER

Owen Foote, Soccer Star

Stephanie Greene

WORLD OF IDEAS

Admitting mistakes, attitude, bullies, betrayal, integrity, loyalty to one's friends, speaking your mind, sportsmanship

Story Synopsis

Owen loves soccer and talks his best friend, Joseph, who is not very good at soccer, into playing on the team. Owen doesn't know what to do when the team bully, Walter, starts to taunt and tease Joseph. He is torn between his love of soccer, standing up for what is right, and being loyal to Joseph.

Who, What, When, and Why

★ Why does Owen betray Joseph and tell Walter that Joseph is not his friend? Is he embarrassed of Joseph's skills?
Why doesn't he stop Walter from teasing Joseph? Is he afraid Walter will start teasing him, too?

★ Why do the children copy Walter? Do they like him?
Do they like him because he is a good soccer player?
Would they like him if he was not good at soccer?
Do you know anyone like Walter?

★ Why does Dave, the coach, make the decision to divide the team into Aliens 1 and Aliens 2? What bothers Owen about the team being divided?
What makes Dave change his mind and admit his mistake?

★ What plan does Joseph have for dealing with Walter's bullying?
Can kids prevent bullies from "having their way" by sticking together?

OWEN FOOTE,
SOCCER STAR

STEPHANIE GREENE
* ILLUSTRATED BY MARTHA WESTON *

READ TOGETHER: GRADES 2–4
READ ALONE: GRADES 3–4+

Souvenir

"It would be great if people played
games for the fun of it, but most
of them don't."

What I Noticed

I liked that Owen's mom trusted him to
figure things out for himself.

What did you notice?

 Quotes

"Nobody can give you wiser advice than yourself."
—CICERO

Look Closer

☆ What makes it hard to know what is the right
thing to do? Do you always know what is the
right thing?
Do you prefer when your parents or a friend
tell you what to do? Why or why not?

☆ Do you like being compared to other kids?
Do you think adults like to be compared
to other adults?

☆ Is it always wrong to give up?
Can giving up sometimes be the right thing to
do?

☆ What do you think about the soccer
advice Clyde gives Owen—to be a "klutz"
and trip Walter by "accident"?

Next

Check out these other titles:

Jake Drake, Know-It-All
BY ANDREW CLEMENTS

Johnny Long Legs
BY MATT CHRISTOPHER

On the Field with . . . Mia Hamm
BY MATT CHRISTOPHER

Morgy Makes His Move
BY MAGGIE LEWIS

Soccer Hero
BY MATT CHRISTOPHER

Soccer Sam
BY JEAN MARZOLLO

The Real Thief

William Steig

WORLD OF IDEAS

Admitting mistakes,
betrayal, envy,
excuses, forgiveness,
injustice, lying,
reputation, self-esteem,
unintended consequences

Story Synopsis

Gawain, the loyal and trusted chief guard of the Royal treasury, alerts the king that some of his jewels are missing. With no clear explanation or evidence, Gawain is falsely accused and flees to the countryside to hide. "The real thief," filled with guilt and shame, struggles to admit his wrongdoings and find the courage to clear his innocent friend.

Who, What, When, and Why

★ Gawain enjoys a wonderful reputation and is well loved by all but is accused of stealing the royal jewels.
Why does everyone believe he stole the jewels?
If Gawain is innocent, why does he run away?

★ Derek doesn't see himself as a criminal and tells himself he was not stealing the precious items, he was only *taking* them. How does this kind of thinking get Derek in trouble?
Why does he steal the jewels?
Does Derek feel good about himself?
Why does Derek decide to confess his crime to Gawain?

★ Gawain does not want Derek to confess his theft to the community, thus keeping the mystery unsolved. He says Derek has been punished enough. Do you think this is fair?

★ Which do you think is more difficult—Derek confessing his crime, or Gawain accepting his friend's weaknesses and forgiving him?

The Real Thief

READ TOGETHER: GRADES 2–4
READ ALONE: GRADES 3–5

 ## Look Closer

☆ Which is more uncomfortable, knowing you did something wrong or having others know you did something wrong? How would you feel if someone was blamed for something you did and you didn't say anything?

☆ What makes a person feel important? Can things make a person feel important?

☆ A good reputation is a long time in the making. How long does it take to get a bad reputation?

 ## Souvenir

"He was able to love them again, but he loved them now in a wiser way, knowing their weakness."

What I Noticed

While I would be hurt by Derek for causing all the problems, I would be more hurt by the community's false accusations and by the king's betrayal.

What did you notice?

 ## Next

Check out these other titles:

The Castle in the Attic
BY ELIZABETH WINTHROP

Frindle
BY ANDREW CLEMENTS

The Gold-Threaded Dress
BY CAROLYN MARSDEN

One Small Dog
BY JOHANNA HURWITZ

The World According to Humphrey
BY BETTY G. BIRNEY

 ## Quotes

"We read that we ought to forgive our enemies; but we do not read that we ought to forgive our friends."
—SIR FRANCIS BACON

The School Mouse

Dick King-Smith

Adventure, apologies,
determination,
inquisitiveness,
love of learning,
pride, strong will,
stubborn

Story Synopsis

Flora is a young mouse who lives in a school with her family. While her brothers and sisters play, Flora sets out to teach herself to read and write. With this knowledge of words, Flora is able to warn her parents of a box marked *poison*!

Who, What, When, and Why

★ Flora chooses not to move with her family because she wants to stay at school and continue her education. Is she determined or stubborn or both?

Why is she inquisitive, and her brothers and sisters are not?

How does Flora's learning to read help save some of her family?

★ Hyacinth bites Buck's nose in retaliation for Buck fighting and injuring her husband, Robin. Why does Flora tell her mother she must apologize directly to Buck and not apologize to her?

What makes it important for Hyacinth to apologize—to appease her conscience, or to make peace within the family?

Why is it difficult for Hyacinth to apologize directly to Buck? Is it her pride or is she just being stubborn?

Do you think Hyacinth is genuinely sorry for what she did?

How does Hyacinth feel once she finally apologizes?

READ TOGETHER: GRADES 2–4
READ ALONE: GRADES 3–4+

Souvenir

"The first and most important thing, for mice or humans, is to learn to read. Once you can do that, there is no limit to what you can get into your heads."

What I Noticed

I never thought how dangerous it could be if you couldn't read the word *poison*. It made me wonder what other words would be dangerous not to be able to read.

What did you notice?

Quotes

"Ignorance is no excuse—it's the real thing."
—IRENE PETER

Look Closer

☆ **Hyacinth tells Flora she has too high of an opinion about herself. Do you agree?**
Do you think you can have too high an opinion of yourself?
What is your opinion of yourself?

☆ **When do stubbornness and determination work for you? When do they work against you?**
Can you be too stubborn? Can you be too determined?

☆ **Why are some people curious and others not? Are you born curious?**
Are you a curious person? Can you be too curious?

☆ **Where does your "thirst for knowledge" come from?**
What would be your biggest disadvantage if you couldn't read?

Next

Check out these other titles:

I'll Meet You at the Cucumbers
BY LILIAN MOORE

Lady Lollipop
BY DICK KING-SMITH

Pee-Wee and Plush
BY JOHANNA HURWITZ

Stargone John
BY ELLEN KINDT MCKENZIE

The Trumpet of the Swan
BY E. B. WHITE

The Silver Balloon

Susan Bonners

WORLD OF IDEAS

Asking for help, curiosity, determination, initiative, shyness, taking risks, unlikely friendship

Story Synopsis

Little does a shy fourth-grader named Gregory know what will happen when he releases a helium-filled balloon into the sky with his name and address attached. A farmer in a faraway state finds the balloon and starts an unusual correspondence with Gregory that leads not only to friendship but also to an exchange of mystery gifts for each to identify.

Who, What, When, and Why

★ How do Gregory and Mr. Mayfield become pen pals?
Do you have a pen pal? Would you want one?

★ What objects do Mr. Mayfield and Gregory send each other? Why do they choose the objects they do?
What makes Gregory so determined to identify the objects Mr. Mayfield sends? Why doesn't he just ask him?

★ Why do you think Gregory sent his wasp nest when it meant so much to him?
Would you be able to send a pen pal your most prized possession?

★ What makes it difficult for Gregory to phone Professor Axelrod?

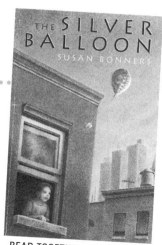

READ TOGETHER: GRADES 2–4

READ ALONE: GRADES 3–4+

 Look Closer

☆ If you were going to send off a balloon and put one clue about yourself in it, what would it be?
What would you want a person to know about you?

☆ Do you get nervous and tongue-tied when you have to talk to people you don't know very well?
Gregory asks, "Why was it easy for other people to ask for help?" Do you find it easy or difficult to ask for help?

Souvenir

"'Just write the way you'd talk to someone,' his mother said."

What I Noticed

The Silver Balloon made me want to put a message in a balloon, send it off and see who I would meet.

What did you notice?

 ## Next

Check out these other titles:

Mysterious Miss Slade
BY DICK KING-SMITH

Owen Foote, Soccer Star
BY STEPHANIE GREENE

The Three Golden Keys
BY PETER SÍS

The Twenty-One Balloons
BY WILLIAM PÈNE DU BOIS

 Quotes

"Research is formalized curiosity. It is poking and prying with a purpose."
—ZORA NEALE HURSTON

Stone Fox

John Reynolds Gardiner

Attitude, belief in yourself, courage, determination, loyalty, perseverance, risk, self-confidence, strong will

Story Synopsis

When Willy's grandfather falls ill, Willy needs to figure out a way to pay the taxes on their farm. With his faithful dog, Searchlight, he enters the National Dogsled Race in hopes of winning the prize money. This race is tough—especially since he is competing with Stone Fox, an impressive and silent Native American, who has never lost a race.

Who, What, When, and Why

★ What words describe Willy—*courageous, determined, risk taker, devoted, loyal, strong willed?*

★ What makes Willy so determined to enter and win the race?
Why does everyone advise Willy to sell the farm?
Why does Doc Smith think Willy should not spend his college money to enter the race?

★ What are Willy's biggest challenges to win the race—the distance, the cold, Searchlight's age, his inexperience, competing against Stone Fox?
Why is Willy convinced he will win the race?
Why did Willy decide to take the risk and cross the lake and possibly fall through the ice? Do you think this was a smart thing to do?

★ Stone Fox refuses to talk to white people because his people have been forced off their land. Why does Stone Fox want to win the race?
What makes Stone Fox such a formidable opponent for Willy?
Why does Stone Fox let Willy win the race?

READING TOGETHER

READ TOGETHER: GRADES 2–4
READ ALONE: GRADES 3–5

Souvenir

"If your teacher don't know—you ask me. If I don't know—you ask the library. If the library don't know—then you've got yourself a good question!"

What I Noticed

I was glad Willy won the race, but Stone Fox, who let Willy cross the finish line first, will always be a winner in my heart.

What did you notice?

 Quotes

"It ain't over till it's over."
—YOGI BERRA

Look Closer

☆ Do you agree with Willy's grandfather who tells him to never accept help unless you can pay for it? How else besides money could you repay someone's help?

☆ Can you accomplish something difficult without believing in yourself?
Is believing in yourself the same as having self-confidence?
What counts more—perseverance or self-confidence?

☆ Who did you think would win the race? Who did you want to win the race?
Are you sorry they both couldn't win?

Next

Check out these other titles:

A Lion to Guard Us
BY CLYDE ROBERT BULLA

Balto and the Great Race
BY ELIZABETH CODY KIMMEL

Because of Winn-Dixie
BY KATE DICAMILLO

Dogteam
BY GARY PAULSEN

A Horn for Louis
BY ERIC KIMMEL

*Nellie Bly:
A Name to Be Reckoned With*
BY STEPHEN KRENSKY

The Stories Julian Tells

Ann Cameron

WORLD OF IDEAS

Fibbing,
new friendship,
siblings,
wishes,
wordplay

Story Synopsis

Julian is a natural-born storyteller. His stories are engaging and wonderful, but not always truthful. With colorful language he is able to spin a tale—sometimes at the expense of his little brother, Huey.

Who, What, When, and Why

★ Why are Julian and Huey hiding under the bed? What do they tell their father happened to the pudding?
Why do they tell their mom they don't want any pudding?

★ Julian fools Huey into thinking that the garden catalog will be full of cats to help make a garden. The catalog arrives, with no cats, and poor Huey is so upset he begins to cry. What does the father tell Huey about catalog cats?

★ Why does Julian eat the fig tree's leaves? Why does Julian apologize to the fig tree for eating its leaves?

★ Why do Gloria and Huey make a kite and attach their list of wishes as a tail?
What are some of their wishes?

READING TOGETHER

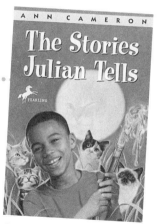

ANN CAMERON
The Stories Julian Tells

READ TOGETHER: GRADES 1–3
READ ALONE: GRADES 2–3+

Souvenir

"The pudding will taste like a whole raft of lemons. It will taste like a night on the sea."

 # Look Closer

☆ In the summer, Julian likes to lie in the grass and look at clouds and eat figs. What do you like to do in the summer? In the winter? In the fall? In the spring? Which is your favorite season?

☆ Have you ever received a tree for a birthday present? Would you want a tree for your birthday?

☆ What is the best thing about having a brother or sister? What annoys you about having a brother or sister?

☆ What would be on your list of wishes? Do you think anyone would be able to guess your wishes? Would you be able to guess a good friend's wishes?

What I Noticed

I don't like it that Julian was teased for having a girl for a friend. I wonder if Gloria would be teased if her friends knew Julian was her friend.

What did you notice?

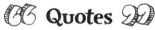 ## Quotes

"The most wasted day of all is that on which we have not laughed."
—SEBASTIEN ROCH NICOLAS CHAMFORT

 # Next

Check out these other titles:

Bailey Goes Camping
BY KEVIN HENKES

The Day I Swapped My Dad for Two Goldfish
BY NEIL GAIMAN

The King Who Rained
FRED GWYNNE

Pictures from Our Vacation
BY LYNNE RAE PERKINS

Stink: The Incredible Shrinking Kid
BY MEGAN MCDONALD

Teach Us, Amelia Bedelia
BY PEGGY PARISH

The Storm

Cynthia Rylant

WORLD OF IDEAS

Courage, destiny, family, friendship, loneliness, purpose, resourcefulness, responsibility

Story Synopsis

Pandora grows weary and lonely as the keeper of a lighthouse. All this changes when after a horrendous storm she rescues a seafaring dog named Seabold. As she nurses him back to health a friendship blossoms and they find companionship. Seabold's decision to return to his life at sea is interrupted when he rescues three orphaned mice. Both Seabold and Pandora nurse them back to health, completing their family.

Who, What, When, and Why

★ Why does Pandora decide to become a lighthouse keeper?
What do lighthouse keepers do?
What doesn't she like about her job?

★ What changes at the lighthouse after Seabold arrives?
How do Pandora and Seabold spend their time together?

★ How does Pandora's commitment to staying at the lighthouse and helping people caught in storms influence Seabold's decision not to return to sea?

★ What changes for Seabold and Pandora with the arrival of the orphaned mice?
Why do the mice make them happy?

READ TOGETHER: GRADES 1–3
READ ALONE: GRADES 2–3+

 Look Closer

☆ Pandora says she knew it was her destiny to become a lighthouse keeper. What do you think is your destiny? Could you substitute the word *purpose* for *destiny*?

☆ What would you do to make your life "count for something"?

☆ Do you like to be alone? What do you like to do when you're alone? What is the difference between being alone and being lonely?

Souvenir

What I Noticed

I like to be alone, but I would not want to live by myself in a lighthouse. I was glad that Pandora met Seabold.

What did you notice?

 Next

Check out these other titles:

Abel's Island
BY WILLIAM STEIG

Animal Family
BY RANDALL JARRELL

Mysterious Miss Slade
BY DICK KING-SMITH

The Story of a Seagull and the Cat Who Taught Her to Fly
BY LUIS SEPÚLVEDA

 **Quotes**

"If you want happiness for a lifetime—help others."
—CHINESE PROVERB

Sun and Spoon

Kevin Henkes

WORLD OF IDEAS

Complicated feelings,
consequences,
death of a grandparent,
family dynamics, guilt,
life goes on,
memories, mistakes

Story Synopsis

After the death of Spoon's grandmother, ten-year-old Spoon is worried that he is going to forget her. To keep his grandmother's memory alive he takes a deck of her cards from his grandfather's home. He didn't ask his grandfather for the cards; he didn't realize his grandfather would miss them. Spoon now has to figure out a way to return his grandmother's cards.

Who, What, When, and Why

★ Spoon doesn't think his grandfather, Pa, will miss the cards because he doesn't seem to want to play cards anymore.

Why does Spoon choose to take his grandmother's deck of playing cards?

Why doesn't he just ask Pa if he can have the cards?

What makes Spoon feel guilty about taking the cards?

Once Pa discovers the cards are missing, why doesn't Spoon just tell him he took them?

Why does Spoon decide not to offer Pa an explanation for the found cards?

What makes him decide to eventually tell Pa that he took the cards?

Why do Pa and Spoon feel better at the end of the story?

KEVIN HENKES
Author of the Newbery Honor Book *Olive's Ocean*

READ TOGETHER: GRADES 3–4
READ ALONE: GRADES 3–5

Souvenir

"It wasn't the most brave thing to do—return the cards without an explanation—but it was all he was capable of at the moment."

 Look Closer

☆ **Do you ever feel like your siblings outshine you?**
Do you ever feel your family doesn't understand you?

☆ **Do you think you ever get too old, or maybe too big, to be scooped up, kissed, and flipped onto your dad's shoulders?**
Maybe the gestures have to change but are you ever too old for the hugs and the kisses?

☆ **Do you have a lucky charm? What makes it lucky?**
If you don't have a lucky charm, why not?

☆ **Do you have something, a memento, that makes you feel close to a person?**
What would you give someone to make them think of you?

What I Noticed

I liked the end of the story when Pa and Spoon are once again playing cards.

What did you notice?

66 Quotes 99

"Pain is part of being alive, and we need to learn that. Pain does not last forever, nor is it necessarily unbearable, and we need to be taught that."
—RABBI HAROLD KUSHNER

Next

Check out these other titles:

Blackberries in the Dark
BY MAVIS JUKES

The Hundred Penny Box
BY SHARON BELL MATHIS

Love, Ruby Lavender
BY DEBORAH WILES

Missing May
BY CYNTHIA RYLANT

Ola's Wake
BY B. J. STONE

Tashi

Anna Fienberg and Barbara Feinberg

Adventures, bravery, cleverness, courage, dragons, imaginary friends, make-believe

Story Synopsis

Jack has a wonderful elfin friend named Tashi, who tells him adventure after adventure after adventure. He is awed by Tashi's stories and his cleverness in outsmarting demons, ghosts, and giants.

Who, What, When, and Why

★ What does Jack learn from Tashi about what to do if you meet a dragon?
Why does the dragon need cheering up?
Why don't dragons like water?
What does Tashi do to trick the last dragon in the world?
What does the dragon see when he looks into the water?

READ TOGETHER: GRADES 1–3
READ ALONE: GRADES 2–3+

Souvenir

"Come and I'll tell you about the time
I tricked the last dragon of all."

What I Noticed

The story made me realize how
dull my life would be if I didn't
believe in what I imagined.

What did you notice?

 **Quotes**

"This is cause for celebration! A human
with imagination!"

—FLORENCE PARRY HEIDE

 Look Closer

☆ Do you have a friend like Tashi? What is
your friend's name?
Would you like to have a friend like Tashi?
What would you name your friend?
Could you make up a story about your
imaginary friend?

☆ Would you keep a friend like Tashi a
secret?
Why would you or why wouldn't you keep
Tashi a secret?

☆ Why is make-believe so fun? Is make-
believe simply purple dogs and pink cats
or imaginary friends and so much more?

Next

Check out these other titles:

The Jamie and Angus Stories
BY ANNE FINE

Jethro Byrd, Fairy Child
BY BOB GRAHAM

Leon and Bob
BY SIMON JAMES

The Lost Flower Children
BY JANET TAYLOR LISLE

McBroom Tells a Lie
BY SID FLEISCHMAN

Moominsummer Madness
BY TOVE JANSSON

Three Terrible Trins

Dick King-Smith

WORLD OF IDEAS

Belief in oneself, bravery, competence, prejudice, snobbery, stereotyping, teamwork

Story Synopsis

After the death of her third husband, Mrs. Gray turns her attention to the education and upbringing of her three children, the trins. With a loving but firm hand she raises them to be the "best" and the "strongest"—to avenge the death of their father. The three mice brothers, ignoring the class system, befriend a lower-class mouse and form a team to fight the cats.

Who, What, When, and Why

★ What are the differences between the four tribes—the Attics, the Ups, the Downs, and the Cellarmice—that live at Orchard Farm? Which tribe was considered superior and which tribe was considered the "lowest of the low"?
What makes some mice superior and some mice the "lowest of the low"?

★ Mrs. Gray brainwashes the trins to become superfighters so they can get rid of the cats and avenge their father's untimely death. What does she tell them to build their confidence?
What is her fitness program?

★ Kevin says his mother told him that Attics were a "stuck-up lot," and Richard tells Kevin that he was told Cellarmice are "the pits." How does getting to know the Attics and the Cellarmice negate what each has been told?
How does Kevin's friendship with the trins help him see himself in a new light?

READING TOGETHER

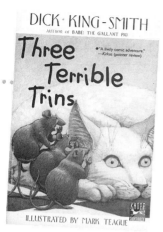

DICK · KING-SMITH
AUTHOR OF BABE: THE GALLANT PIG

Three Terrible Trins

"A lively comic adventure."
—Kirkus (pointer review)

KNOPF

ILLUSTRATED BY MARK TEAGUE

READ TOGETHER: GRADES 2–4
READ ALONE: GRADES 3–5

 Look Closer

☆ If you believe you are capable, are you capable? How important is it to believe in yourself?

☆ Are first impressions reliable?

☆ Why is it easy to stereotype people in a group? What changes when you get to know them as individuals?

☆ What is your definition of a snob? What is most bothersome about a snob? Why are some people snobs?

Souvenir

"Attics by birth the trins may have been, but they made it quite clear to anyone and everyone that they much disliked the old snobbish clan system."

What I Noticed

The story made me realize how ridiculous it is to stereotype a person based on where they live.

What did you notice?

 **Next**

Check out these other titles:

The Araboolies of Liberty Street
BY SAM SWOPE

The Dragonling
BY JACKIE FRENCH KOLLER

Pet of the Met
BY DON FREEMAN

The Sneetches and Other Stories
BY DR. SEUSS

 **Quotes**

"Tell a man he is brave and you help him become so."
—THOMAS CARLYLE

The Trouble with Cats

Martha Freeman

Story Synopsis

Not only does Holly have to adjust to a new stepfather, a new home, and a new school but she is also expected to share her bedroom with four crazy cats. Holly, a character full of can-do attitude, adjusts to her new living situation and new school, but not without a few complications along the way.

Who, What, When, and Why

★ **What bothers Holly about the cats?**
Why is it difficult for Holly to share her room with the cats?
What do the cats do that make Holly late for school?
In what other ways do they make Holly's life miserable?

★ **Why does William expect Holly to clean up the cats' throw-up?**
Do you think it is fair of William to expect Holly to clean it up?
Do you think Holly has a bad attitude when she refuses to clean it up?
Do you think it is wrong of Holly to run away?

★ **Why does Holly feel that nobody understands her? Have you ever felt like Holly?**
How does Mary's story about her stepfather change Holly's perspective about her stepfather?

The Trouble with Cats

by Martha Freeman
illustrated by Cat Bowman Smith

READ TOGETHER: GRADES 2–4
READ ALONE: GRADES 3–4+

 **Look Closer**

☆ Do you think there is such a thing as a perfect school or a perfect life?

☆ Are you good at adjusting to new situations? Has there been a situation that was difficult for you to adjust to?

☆ What is a "no-nonsense look"? Do you ever get a no-nonsense look? Can you ignore a no-nonsense look?

☆ How does hearing someone else's story change your perspective and attitude?

Souvenir

"It was the first time in a while I had listened to anybody except me."

What I Noticed

How many times have I felt that my life was "awful" and then I heard someone else's story and realized my life is pretty good?

What did you notice?

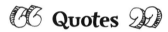 **Quotes**

"The bamboo that bends is stronger than the oak that resists."
—JAPANESE PROVERB

Next

Check out these other titles:

Clementine
BY SARA PENNYPACKER

Mysterious Miss Slade
BY DICK KING-SMITH

One Small Dog
BY JOHANNA HURWITZ

Piper Reed, Navy Brat
BY KIMBERLY WILLIS HOLT

Scooter
BY VERA B. WILLIAMS

Tooter Pepperday
BY JERRY SPINELLI

The Whipping Boy

Sid Fleischman

WORLD OF IDEAS

Class discrimination, mistaken identity, power of knowledge, self-reliance, unlikely friendship

Story Synopsis

Prince Horace is spoiled and obnoxious; his nickname is Prince Brat. The rule is a prince cannot be punished, so in his place Jemmy, a poor rat-catcher's son, is whipped for the prince's bad behavior. The prince decides to run away and takes Jemmy with him. In their attempt to make it back to the castle safely, they find themselves captured by two cutthroats and their roles are reversed.

Who, What, When, and Why

★ What words describe Jemmy—*intelligent, quick thinking, clever, self-reliant*? Where does Jemmy learn these traits? Do you think he would have these traits if his life had been easier?
Where does Jemmy learn to read?
Why doesn't Jemmy want to return to his life in the sewers?

★ Why is Jemmy able to convince Cutwater and Hold-Your-Nose Billy that he is the prince and the prince is the whipping boy?
What advantage does Jemmy have over Cutwater and Hold-Your-Nose Billy?

★ What words describe the Prince Brat—*spoiled, ignorant, irresponsible, unable to rely on himself*?
Were does the prince learn these traits? Do you think he would have these traits if his life had been harder?

★ Does Prince Brat return to the castle as a brat? Does Jemmy return as a whipping boy?

READ TOGETHER: GRADES 2–4
READ ALONE: GRADES 3–4+

Souvenir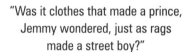

"Was it clothes that made a prince,
Jemmy wondered, just as rags
made a street boy?"

 # Look Closer

☆ If you grow up in luxury, having everything done for you, can you learn to be
independent and self-reliant?
How do you learn to be independent and
self-reliant?

☆ Can you be friends with someone who
comes from a very "different way of life"?
Once you get to know that person, how
different are they?
What makes having a friend from a "different way of life" interesting?

☆ Could you imagine not being able to
read or write? What would your life look
like?
How easy would it be for someone to fool
you if you couldn't read or write?

What I Noticed

I loved when the king said that next
time the boys decide to run away, he
would like to go with them.

What did you notice?

 Quotes

*"The best place to find a helping hand is at
the end of your own arm."*
—SWEDISH PROVERB

Next

Check out these other titles:

The Door in the Wall
BY MARGUERITE DE ANGELI

The King's Equal
BY KATHERINE PATERSON

Lady Lollipop
BY DICK KING-SMITH

The Wish Giver
BY BILL BRITTAIN

The World According to Humphrey
BY BETTY G. BIRNEY

The World According to Humphrey

Betty G. Birney

WORLD OF IDEAS

Empathy, encouragement, first impressions, knowing the full story before making a judgment, making a difference

Story Synopsis

Ms. Mac, the substitute teacher, brings Humphrey, a hamster, to live in room 26. The teachers, the principal, and the schoolchildren all love Humphrey, but when Mrs. Brisbane comes back to teach, she is less than enthusiastic about the class pet. Humphrey, with his big heart, brings out the best in people and discovers he has an important role to play in helping his classmates and teacher.

Who, What, When, and Why

★ How does Humphrey's presence make a positive difference for everyone?

★ At school, everybody listens to Mr. Morales, the school principal. What does Humphrey discover during his weekend at Mr. Morales's home?

★ A.J. talks "loud, loud, loud" at school. What does Humphrey discover during his weekend at A.J's home?

★ Garth disrupts the class, and he is angry that everyone loves Humphrey and nobody likes him. What does Mrs. Brisbane discover about Garth's family that explains his behavior?

★ Why does Humphrey think Mrs. Brisbane doesn't want to take him home? What does Humphrey discover about Mrs. Brisbane during the Thanksgiving weekend?
What happens during his stay that helps Mr. Brisbane make a new start?

READING TOGETHER

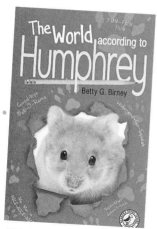

Betty G. Birney

READ TOGETHER: GRADES 2–5
READ ALONE: GRADE 4+

Souvenir

"I found out kids have problems and so do teachers and principals. Sometimes all people need is a little encouragement. Most of all, I learned that one small hamster really can make a big difference."

 Look Closer

☆ If Humphrey came to your house for a weekend, what would be his first impression? What would he notice?

What does your room look like? Is it messy or clean or somewhere in between?

Are you helpful around the house? Who is the most helpful person in the family?

Does your family laugh a lot? Argue a lot? Disagree a lot?

Who has a temper in your family? Who is the most easygoing?

Who laughs the most? Who cries the most?

☆ Would Humphrey know "everything" about your family after his weekend stay?

How could Humphrey's presence make a positive difference?

What I Noticed

I would love to be able to spend a weekend with so many different families, and I wonder what I would observe.

What did you notice?

Quotes

"Every path has its puddle."
—ENGLISH PROVERB

 Next

Check out these other titles:

Clementine
BY SARA PENNYPACKER

Dominic
BY WILLIAM STEIG

Gooney Bird Greene
BY LOIS LOWRY

The Van Gogh Café
BY CYNTHIA RYLANT

The Year of Miss Agnes

Kirkpatrick Hill

WORLD OF IDEAS

Dedication, disability, expectations, learning styles, making a difference, pragmatism, respect, self-sufficiency

Story Synopsis

In 1948, Agnes Sutterfield arrived in frontier Alaska to teach in a one-room schoolhouse. Miss Agnes introduced the children to wonderful stories and faraway places and respected and appreciated their customs. She didn't even mind the smell of fish that the children brought for lunch.

Who, What, When, and Why

★ **What words describe Miss Agnes**—*strong, accepting, pragmatic, expecting the best, sensible, understanding*?
Why are Miss Agnes's books more interesting than the Dick and Jane books?
How does she show them they can use math outside the classroom?
Why does she insist that Bakko, who is deaf, attend school?
Why does Miss Agnes return for a second year when her intention had been to stay for one year? Do you think Miss Agnes is still there?

★ **What words describe the mom**—*practical, traditional, handy, self-sufficient, overwhelmed, impatient, loving, not understanding*?
Why doesn't she want Bakko to attend school? Why does she change her mind?
Grandpa says that a hard-luck person can get kind of mean. How do hardships make the mom "kind of mean"?

READ TOGETHER: GRADES 2–4
READ ALONE: GRADES 3–5

 Souvenir

"You have to keep learning all your life."

What I Noticed

I liked how Miss Agnes showed her students that they could be whatever they wanted to be. She gave them the gift of possibilities.

What did you notice?

 Quotes

"Tell me and I'll forget; show me and I may remember; involve me and I'll understand."

—CHINESE PROVERB

 **Look Closer**

☆ Do you think school should be fun?
How would you arrange the desks? Where would you put the teacher's desk?
Would you give grades? Would you give tests? Why are grades and tests given?
Would you play music in your classroom? What kind of music?
Would you read aloud to your students? What book would you choose?

☆ Miss Agnes said everyone was good at something. What are you good at?

☆ How difficult would it be to move to a totally different environment with different weather, food, attitudes, and ways of doing things?
What would make it difficult? What would make it interesting?
Would you want to do this? What would you miss most from your home?

Next

Check out these other titles:

Bird Boy
BY ELIZABETH STARR HILL

The Indian School
BY GLORIA WHELAN

Mary on Horseback
BY ROSEMARY WELLS

The Most Beautiful Place in the World
BY ELEANOR CAMERON

The Secret School
BY AVI

The 13 Clocks

James Thurber

WORLD OF IDEAS

Good and evil,
kindness, laughter,
magic spells,
wordplay

Story Synopsis

This is a tale of an evil duke and his niece, the beautiful princess (who really isn't his niece), who live in a dark, gloomy castle. Xingu, a wandering minstrel (who is really Prince Zorn of Zorna), wanders into town declaring he is going to marry the princess. With the aid of a magical creature, the Golux (who is really Listen), the prince sets off to try to pass the duke's impossible test in hopes of marrying the princess and living happily ever after.

Who, What, When, and Why

★ Why does the duke make it nearly impossible for Saralinda's suitors to marry her? Is he on the side of good or evil?

★ The Golux makes things up and forgets things. The duke hires him to be his spy, and he also befriends Xingu. Is he on the side of good or evil?

★ Why does King Gwain gift Hagga with the power to weep jewels instead of tears after she frees his foot from a trap?
Why does the king turn the couple that laughed at him into grasshoppers? Is he punishing laughter when it is at someone else's expense?
Why does the king make the jewels of sorrow last forever but the jewels of laughter turn into tears in a fortnight?

★ Are the jewels Prince Zorn brings the duke jewels from laughter or jewels from tears?
How do these jewels defeat the duke?

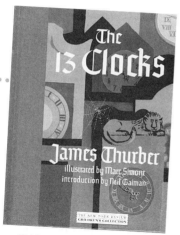

READ TOGETHER: GRADES 3–5
READ ALONE: GRADE 4+

Look Closer

☆ If you cry over everything and anything, do your tears become meaningless? Do you think tears can dry up?

☆ What would you tell Hagga to make her cry? Do you cry easily?

☆ What would you tell Hagga to make her laugh? Do you laugh easily?

☆ Which is stronger, laughter or sorrow? What happens when you have one without the other?

☆ Have you ever wondered …
How would forever smell?
What does silence sound like?
Can you slay the sound of time?

Souvenir

"Remember laughter. You'll need it even in the blessed isles of Ever After."

What I Noticed

I am usually annoyed and easily confused with stories when up is down and down is up, but I thoroughly enjoyed this story.

What did you notice?

Next

Check out these other titles:

The Boggart
BY SUSAN COOPER

The Bookstore Mouse
BY PEGGY CHRISTIAN

Bright Shadow
BY AVI

The Devil's Storybook
BY NATALIE BABBITT

Midnight Magic
BY AVI

Shadow Spinner
BY SUSAN FLETCHER

 Quotes

"Always be a little kinder than necessary."
—SIR JAMES M. BARRIE

All Alone in the Universe

Lynne Rae Perkins

WORLD OF IDEAS

First impressions, friendships lost and made, growing up, heartache, kindness, loneliness, self-awareness, transitions

Story Synopsis

Debbie and Maureen have been best friends since third grade. When Maureen starts spending more time with their classmate Glenna, Debbie becomes annoyed—she doesn't like Glenna and feels she is taking her friend away from her. Debbie begins to feel pushed out of the friendship and "all alone in the universe."

Who, What, When, and Why

★ Debbie and Maureen do not have a noisy breakup, but during the summer they begin to drift apart. What causes the rift in their friendship? Does Maureen understand how Debbie feels?

★ Debbie's first impressions of her neighbor, Marie Prbyczka, comes from who Marie hangs out with, how she dresses, and the appearance of her house. What do those things tell her about Marie? What changes after she gets to know Marie?

★ Miss Epler, her English teacher, tells Debbie that she should be angry at the right person. Who should Debbie be angry at—Glenna for taking her friend away, Maureen for going off with Glenna, or herself for outgrowing her friendship with Maureen?

★ What does Debbie begin to understand about herself and her friendship with Maureen after she becomes friendly with Alice and Patty?

READING TOGETHER

READ TOGETHER: GRADES 4–6
READ ALONE: GRADE 5+

Souvenir

"Don't wait for someone else to make it [your life] happen. You have to make it happen."

 Look Closer

☆ Have you ever felt betrayed by a friend? Is betrayal the same as disappointment or hurt?
Can someone take a friend away from you?

☆ Can you outgrow a friendship? Have you ever drifted apart from a friend?
Was it because of something your friend did or another reason?

☆ Have you ever told yourself a situation wasn't happening because it was too uncomfortable to face? Did it work?

☆ Have you ever tried to name the good qualities of someone you do not like?

What I Noticed

The story made me see there is life after losing a friend, and there are new friends waiting to be made.

What did you notice?

 Quotes

"Only I can change my life. No one can do it for me."
—CAROL BURNETT

Next

Check out these other titles:

Because of Winn-Dixie
BY KATE DICAMILLO

Gracie's Girl
BY ELLEN WITTLINGER

Jennifer, Hecate, Macbeth, William McKinley, and Me, Elizabeth
BY E. L. KONIGSBURG

My Louisiana Sky
BY KIMBERLY WILLIS HOLT

My One Hundred Adventures
BY POLLY HORVATH

The Van Gogh Café
BY CYNTHIA RYLANT

The Bad Beginning

Lemony Snicket

Story Synopsis

What starts out unfortunate just gets worse for the three Baudelaire children. Recently orphaned, they find themselves in the custody of their closest living relative, Count Olaf, who is determined to get his hands on their money. One unfortunate event after another challenges the three resourceful children in their attempts to thwart the count's plans.

Who, What, When, and Why

★ What words describe Count Olaf—*greedy, conniving, devious, shrewd, sneaky*?
When do you become suspicious of Count Olaf's motives?
What is his plan to get the children's money?

★ Why is Justice Strauss unable to believe that Count Olaf is up to something? How does her desire to perform onstage cloud her thinking?
Or is it just one more unfortunate event in the life of the Baudelaire children that Justice Strauss always wanted to perform onstage?

★ Why doesn't Mr. Poe help the children after he hears their complaints about living with Count Olaf? Is he too busy to get involved or does he just not care?
Or is it just one more unfortunate event in the life of the Baudelaire children that Mr. Poe is the executor for their parents' estate?

READ TOGETHER: GRADES 4–6

READ ALONE: GRADE 5+

Souvenir

"Sometimes, just saying that you hate something, and having someone agree with you, can make you feel better about a terrible situation."

 # Look Closer

☆ Who would you choose to be in an "unfortunate event" with? What resources, strengths, and attributes would they bring to this unfortunate event?
Who would you not want to go through an unfortunate event with?

☆ When faced with an unfortunate event, is your go-to attitude "keep your chin up" or "woe is me"?
Where does "woe is me" get you? Where does "keep your chin up" get you?

☆ Do you need happy endings in the stories you read? Will you not read a book if you know the ending is sad?
Can you think of a story where the ending is both happy and sad?

What I Noticed

I like how the author explains what all the big words mean. There should be more books like this!

What did you notice?

 ## Quotes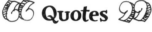

"Flattery is like cologne water, to be smelt of, not swallowed."
—JOSH BILLINGS

 # Next

Check out these other titles:

The 13 Clocks
BY JAMES THURBER

James and the Giant Peach
BY ROALD DAHL

From the Mixed-Up Files of Mrs. Basil E. Frankweiler
BY E. L. KONIGSBURG

The Mysterious Benedict Society
BY TRENTON LEE STEWART

The Westing Game
BY ELLEN RASKIN

The Wolves of Willoughby Chase
BY JOAN AIKEN

Bridge to Terabithia

Katherine Paterson

WORLD OF IDEAS

Bullies, consequences,
death, empathy,
fear, friendship,
life-changing experience,
life goes on,
self-awareness

Story Synopsis

Jess Aarons, a middle child, and Leslie Burke, the only daughter of two writers from New York City, become best friends in rural Virginia. Together they create Terabithia, a magical kingdom accessible only by a rope swing over a creek bed. A tragedy occurs that changes their lives forever when Jess visits a museum in the city and Leslie ventures to Terabithia alone.

Who, What, When, and Why

★ Jess and Leslie come from two very different families; nevertheless, they become close friends. What words describe Jess—*fearful, artistic, responsible, provincial*?
What words describe Leslie—*fearless, imaginative, well read, worldly*?
Why do Jess and Leslie become friends? What do they have in common?

★ Janice Avery, the class bully, steals May Belle's Twinkies, and in revenge, Jess and Leslie make a fool of her. What do they do to humiliate her?
Why do Jess's and Leslie's feelings toward Janice change when Leslie discovers Janice crying in the girls' bathroom? Do they now have empathy for her?

★ Jess and Leslie create Terabithia, where everything seemed possible and where nothing could defeat them. How did Terabithia help Jess get a different sense of himself? How did Leslie help Jess be his best self?
Why does Jess suggest May Belle might be the new queen of Terabithia? How does this carry on the spirit of Terabithia?

READ TOGETHER: GRADES 4–6
READ ALONE: GRADE 5+

Souvenir

"It was Leslie who had taken him from the cow pasture into Terabithia and turned him into a king."

What I Noticed

I liked that Jess wanted May Belle to be the new queen of Terabithia. I know that Leslie would have liked that, too.

What did you notice?

 Quotes

"Death ends a life, not a relationship."
—ROBERT BENCHLEY

 # Look Closer

☆ What are you looking for in a friend? Do you look for friends that make you feel understood, appreciated, respected, good about yourself, and special?
Do you think a friend can help you be your best self?
Do you think a friend can help you see a different side of yourself?

☆ How does knowing the whole story influence the way you understand a person?
Does not knowing the whole story lead to misunderstandings?

☆ How can you keep a person's memory alive? By telling stories about that person, by emulating their deeds, by following their ideals?
In your family do you have traditions and rituals that keep a person's memory alive, such as lighting a candle, planting a tree, or saying a special prayer?

Next

Check out these other titles:

Dovey Coe
BY FRANCES O'ROARK DOWELL

Love, Ruby Lavender
BY DEBORAH WILES

Mick Harte Was Here
BY BARBARA PARK

On My Honor
BY MARION DANE BAUER

The Castle in the Attic

Elizabeth Winthrop

WORLD OF IDEAS

Admitting mistakes, belief in yourself, challenges, chivalry, confronting fear, courage, good and evil, knights, quests, unintended consequences

Story Synopsis

Mrs. Phillips, William's nanny, decides to move back to England and gives him a wooden castle that has been in her family for generations. William, so upset with her departure, rashly shrinks Mrs. Phillips to the size of a toy knight so she will not return to England. In order to bring her back, he must shrink himself, enter the castle, and overthrow the evil magician Alastor.

Who, What, When, and Why

★ What does William regret about using the magic token to prevent Mrs. Phillips from returning to England? What bothers you most about what William did to Mrs. Phillips?
Is Mrs. Phillips more angry or disappointed in William?

★ What challenges does William face on his quest to help Sir Simon reclaim his kingdom and get the magic token from Alastor?
What makes William able to resist the temptations he meets on his quest to overthrow Alastor? Is it the knowledge he has done something wrong and needs to undo it, or is it that he gains confidence in himself?

★ Magic can be used for purposes of good or evil. What does Alastor use his magic for?

READ TOGETHER: GRADES 3–5
READ ALONE: GRADE 4+

Souvenir

"A truly courageous person is the one who must first conquer fear within himself."

 # Look Closer

☆ **Why do some things need to stay private?**
What kinds of things do you have to figure out for yourself that you would not be willing to share with a friend?

☆ **Can someone be your good luck charm?**
Do you have a good luck charm?
If you believe that someone or something brings you luck, does that make it so?

☆ **What builds self-confidence—**
accomplishments, overcoming challenges, praise, achievements, encouragements?
Where does confidence come from, yourself or others? Can somebody give you confidence?

☆ **If you looked into a mirror that had the ability to show you who you really are, what would you like the mirror show you?**

What I Noticed

I was shocked that William shrunk Mrs. Phillips and was so thankful he was able to rescue her, defeat Alastor, and return the kingdom to Sir Simon, the rightful heir.

What did you notice?

 ## Quotes

"*They are able because they think they are able.*"
—VIRGIL

 # Next

Check out these other titles:

The Door in the Wall
BY MARGUERITE DE ANGELI

The Children of Green Knowe
BY L. M. BOSTON

Half Magic
BY EDWARD EAGER

The Indian in the Cupboard
BY LYNNE REID BANKS

The Land of Green Ginger
BY NOEL LANGLEY

Code Talker

Joseph Bruchac

Story Synopsis

Ned Begay, a Navajo Indian, left his reservation to attend boarding school to learn English and the "American way." Speaking the Navajo language was forbidden at school. When the Japanese bombed Pearl Harbor and the war in the Pacific erupted, Ned enlisted in the U.S. Marines. He and a select group of Navajos were trained to transmit information in battle using a code based on their native tongue.

WORLD OF IDEAS

Attitude, discrimination, courage, Native American culture, Navajo code talkers, Pearl Harbor, prejudice, pride in heritage, self-reliance, survival skills

Who, What, When, and Why

★ What is unjust about the way the students are treated at school? How does the way they are treated insult their native culture?
What is ironic about the school's attempt to destroy the Navajo language?

★ What words describe Ned—*focused, intent on excelling, stubborn, true to his traditions*?
The Navajos believe in the importance of balance and peace in the sacred ways. In what ways does the Navajo culture help Ned survive?

★ How did the following make the war in the Pacific so difficult?
The Imperial Japanese Army Instructional Manual set five rules of combat, one of which was that you could never surrender.
Japanese pilots who flew suicide missions (kamikaze) thought they were flying with the holy wind.
Many Japanese citizens tried to speak out against the war, but were imprisoned by the Thought Police, a powerful military organization.

A Novel About
the Navajo Marines of World War Two

READ TOGETHER: GRADE 5+
READ ALONE: GRADE 6+

 # Look Closer

☆ Ned prays, "Let me have clear thoughts, clear speech, and a good path to walk this day." You could call Ned's prayer a meditation. What would be your personal mediation to begin each day?

☆ "Finding your balance" is important to Navajo culture. What rituals do you have that help you find balance and get back to the core of who you are and what you believe?
Can you make difficult choices when you are not "in balance"?

Souvenir

"Never think that war is a good thing . . . though it may be necessary."

Next

Check out these other titles:

Hatchet
BY GARY PAULSEN

The Invisible Thread
BY YOSHIKO UCHIDA

George Washington, Spymaster
BY THOMAS B. ALLEN

The Life and Death of Crazy Horse
BY RUSSELL FREEDMAN

Navajo Code Talkers
BY NATHAN AASENG

The War Prayer
BY MARK TWAIN (6+)

What I Noticed

This book made me realize that people need beliefs and rituals that support their well-being.

What did you notice?

 # Quotes

"A brave man is seldom unkind."
—PRETTY-SHIELD, CROW MEDICINE WOMAN

Dear Mr. Henshaw

Beverly Cleary

Broken promises,
disappointment,
divorce, new kid in town,
perspective, unreliable

Story Synopsis

In his letters to Mr. Henshaw, his favorite author, ten-year-old Leigh reveals his challenges in coping with his parents' divorce, being the new boy in school, and trying to find his own place in the world.

Who, What, When, and Why

★ Why does Mr. Henshaw respond to Leigh's letter with a list of questions? Is he curious about Leigh or are the questions meant for Leigh to know himself better?
What does he learn about himself by answering Mr. Henshaw's questions? Why does writing to Mr. Henshaw and writing in his diary make Leigh feel better?

★ Leigh is sad and angry about his parents' divorce, and he worries that he may have caused it. What bothers Leigh about his dad? In what ways does Leigh's dad disappoint him?
What words describe his dad—*hurtful, disappointing, insensitive, unreliable*? Is he a bad person?

★ How does Leigh feel when Barry asks him to come to his house to rig up an alarm?
What does Mr. Findlay mean when he asks Leigh, "Who wants to be friends with someone who scowls all the time?'

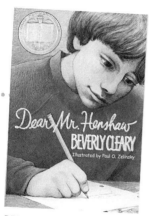

READ TOGETHER: GRADES 4–6
READ ALONE: GRADE 5+

Souvenir

"Whenever I watch the waves, I always feel that no matter how bad things seem, life will still go on."

What I Noticed

I respected Leigh's mom for telling Leigh that his dad was not a bad man.

What did you notice?

 Quotes

"Disappointment is the nurse of wisdom."
—BAYLE ROCHE

 # Look Closer

☆ What qualities do you think are the most important in a dad?
What qualities do you think are the most important in a mom?

☆ How would you answer the questions Mr. Henshaw sent Leigh—Who are you? What do you look like? What is your family like? Who are your friends? What bothers you? What do you wish?

☆ Are you surprised that Leigh, who is a boy, keeps a diary? Do you think diaries are just for girls? Is there another way to keep track of your most personal and secret thoughts?

☆ The story ends on a sad and not-so-sad note. Did you think Leigh's parents were going to get back together?

Next

Check out these other titles:

Blackberries in the Dark
BY MAVIS JUKES

Every Living Thing
BY CYNTHIA RYLANT

The Graduation of Jake Moon
BY BARBARA PARK

Harriet the Spy
BY LOUISE FITZHUGH

Notes from a Liar and Her Dog
BY GENNIFER CHOLDENKO

One Small Dog
BY JOHANNA HURWITZ

Dominic

William Steig

Story Synopsis

Dominic, an adventurous dog, leaves his home to see the world, taking only an assortment of hats and his piccolo. Along the way he encounters and befriends many animals, gaining and sharing riches with his new friends. During this adventure he learns about the world and himself and eventually tackles the notorious Doomsday gang.

WORLD OF IDEAS

Adventure, courage, death, fate, generosity, good versus evil, making a difference, tolerance

Who, What, When, and Why

★ What makes Dominic decide to leave home and choose one particular road over the other? Do you think he chose the "right" road?
What words describe Dominic—*adventurous, generous, curious, kind, empathetic, smart, independent, fair, noble*?
What do you most like about Dominic? Why?

★ Why does he get involved with the different animals he meets on his journey? Is he just a generous creature?
Would you have helped free the yellowjacket caught inside a spider's web?
Would you have swept the floor of a sick badger's house?
Would you have given away your jewels?

★ What made Dominic so determined to rid the world of the Doomsday gang? Did he just not like them? Did he not like the way they treated everyone? Or did he think it was important to fight evil?

READING TOGETHER

WILLIAM STEIG
A Caldecott Medal Winner and Newbery Honor Author

Dominic

Dominic is off to see the world!

READ TOGETHER: GRADES 3–5
READ ALONE: GRADE 4+

 Look Closer

☆ How much adventure do you need in life? How open are you to new adventures?

☆ Dominic chooses not to know his future. Would you want to know your future?

☆ Do you agree with Dominic that you cannot be happy with the good unless you fight the bad?

Souvenir

"Conversation with you has broadened my horizons."

What I Noticed

I liked when Dominic played his piccolo for the mice who were having a moonlit dance in the tall grasses. I also liked that he gave a diamond necklace to Elijah Hogg.

What did you notice?

 Quotes

"Destiny is no matter of chance. It is a matter of choice. It is not a thing to be waited for; it is a thing to be achieved."

—WILLIAM JENNINGS BRYAN

Next

Check out these other titles:

The Lemming Condition
BY ALAN ARKIN

The Little Prince
BY ANTOINE DE SAINT-EXUPERY

Perloo the Bold
BY AVI

The Search for Delicious
BY NATALIE BABBITT

The Tale of Despereaux
BY KATE DICAMILLO

The Tale of Tales
BY TONY MITTON

Dovey Coe

Frances O'Roark Dowell

Bullies, disability, humiliation, life-changing experience, murder, responsibility, self-reliance, speaking your mind, unintended consequences, vengeance

Story Synopsis

Dovey Coe lives in the mountains of North Carolina with her parents, her beautiful older sister, Caroline, and her little brother, Amos, who is deaf. Twelve-year-old Dovey has no problem speaking her mind, and everybody knows she hates Parnell Caraway, Caroline's rich boyfriend. When Parnell is found dead, Dovey is accused of murder and finds herself on trial for her life.

Who, What, When, and Why

★ Is Parnell a bully or just someone who always wants his own way? Is there a difference?
How did Parnell get to be the person he is? His mom says Parnell was difficult and spoiled as a child. Would this account for his behavior?

★ What words describe Caroline—*pretty, flirtatious, ambitious, naive*?
How does Caroline use her looks to manipulate people and get what she wants?
What bothers Caroline about Parnell's proposal of marriage? Why does her refusal humiliate him?

★ How does Dovey prove her innocence?

★ Dovey says she doesn't blame Caroline for the "whole mess" and knows it isn't exactly her fault. In what ways does Dovey blame Caroline?
In what ways did Dovey inflame the situation? What portion of the responsibility lies with her?

READ TOGETHER: GRADE 5+
READ ALONE: GRADE 6+

Look Closer

☆ Do you know people who take advantage of their looks to get their way? How do you feel about people who do that? Do men and women both play this "game"?

☆ What does humiliation do to a person?

☆ Does being rich mean that you get whatever you want? Does being rich make you happy? Does being rich entitle you to treat people any way you want? Does being rich mean you are better than other people?

Souvenir

"Well, I'll tell you, honey, partly it's because we tried to raise you children so that when you came of age you could make your own decisions in a clearheaded fashion, whether we agreed with your decision or not."

Next

Check out these other titles:

A Long Way from Chicago
BY RICHARD PECK

The Boy in the Burning House
BY TIM WYNNE-JONES (6+)

Running Out of Time
BY MARGARET PETERSON HADDIX

To Kill a Mockingbird
BY HARPER LEE (7+)

Tuck Everlasting
BY NATALIE BABBITT

What I Noticed

The story makes me think about how dangerous it is to embarrass and humiliate a person.

What did you notice?

 **Quotes**

"To have courage for whatever comes in life—everything lies in that."
—TERESA OF AVILA

Frindle

Andrew Clements

Integrity,
motives,
pranks,
pushing the limits,
unintended consequences

Story Synopsis

Nick Allen is a clever and very likeable fifth-grader. His teacher, Mrs. Granger, loves words and the dictionary, and when Nick decides to substitute the word *frindle* for the word *pen*, his "prank" sets off a chain of events that quickly moves beyond his control.

Who, What, When, and Why

★ Nick would not be on a list of the really bad kids, the really smart kids, or the really good kids. What list would Nick be on? Is he a troublemaker? What list would you be on?

★ Why does Nick substitute the word *frindle* for *pen*? Is this a prank, a game, a test of wills, or what? If it starts out as a game, how does it change?

★ Why does Mrs. Chatham say Nick is showing a lack of respect for authority? What do Nick's mom and dad think of the situation? Do they agree with Mrs. Chatham?

★ What explanation does Mrs. Granger give Nick for the reason she stopped being angry about him substituting the word *frindle* for *pen*? Does your opinion of Mrs. Granger change when you read her letter to Nick?

READ TOGETHER: GRADES 3–5
READ ALONE: GRADE 4 +

Souvenir

"A person can watch the sunrise, but he cannot slow it down or stop it or make it go backward ... Like the sunrise, some things just have to happen—and all you can really do is watch."

 ## Look Closer

☆ The children think using the word *frindle* is fun and didn't want to make the teachers mad. If fun is had at someone else's expense, is it fun?

☆ Nick realizes that being a hero has a price and is not a free ride. How about being popular, the class clown, or the class bully? Do these all have a price?

☆ Nick says he doesn't know how to stop everyone from using the word *frindle*. Have you ever been in a situation that got out of hand?

☆ What is a prank—a game, a trick, or a joke? Why do people play pranks? Are the motives ever "good"?
Can you control the outcome of a prank?

What I Noticed

I was impressed with Mrs. Granger's integrity, and I would like to think that I would have the courage to admit I was wrong.

What did you notice?

Next

Check out these other titles:

The Castle in the Attic
BY ELIZABETH WINTHROP

Harriet the Spy
BY LOUISE FITZHUGH

The Real Thief
BY WILLIAM STEIG

The Trumpet of the Swan
BY E. B. WHITE

 ## Quotes

"Words are all we have."
—SAMUEL BECKETT

The Graduation of Jake Moon

Barbara Park

Acceptance,
Alzheimer's disease,
attitude,
"emotional roller coaster,"
empathy, growing up,
humor, perspective,
responsibility

Story Synopsis

Jake and his grandfather, Skelly, are close and have lived together with his mom since Jake was a baby. When Jake is in eighth grade, his grandfather starts to act strange in front of his friends. He is embarrassed when Skelly looks for his socks in the refrigerator and can't remember names. The love Jake feels for his grandfather is tested by his embarrassment and the overwhelming responsibilities of caring for Skelly.

Who, What, When, and Why

★ When Skelly develops Alzheimer's disease, Jake has to be the grown-up, responsible for much of his care. How does his love of, devotion to, and responsibility for Skelly spiral into embarrassment, resentment, anger, and humiliation?
Life with Skelly is up and down and unpredictable. How does this put Jake on an "emotional roller coaster"?

★ What changes between Jake and James after Skelly's "great adventure"?
Would James be able to understand what it was like to live and care for Skelly day after day when he only saw him once a week?
What does Jake come to understand when James takes Skelly for a walk and offers to bring along Skelly's grocery cart?

★ Why does Jake change his mind and invite Skelly to his graduation?
Are you surprised at how Jake handles the fiasco?

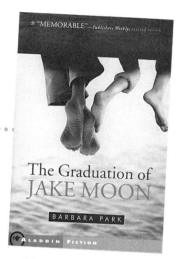

The Graduation of
JAKE MOON

BARBARA PARK

ALADDIN FICTION

READ TOGETHER: GRADE 5+
READ ALONE: GRADE 6+

Souvenir

"It was one of those moments that can make you smile and break your heart at the same time."

Look Closer

☆ What would it feel like to confront something that was not going to be "rip-roaringly happy," and probably wasn't going to be "okay" either?" What makes it hard to accept a situation that you can't change?

☆ Jake is only fourteen years old. Do you think the mom expects too much from Jake? Why or why not?

☆ Why, when people feel embarrassed, humiliated, or overwhelmed, do they often withdraw? Does this protect them from difficult feelings? Does it help them "save face"? Does it give a person time so they can learn to cope? Can you withdraw forever?

What I Noticed

I really liked and admired how Jake found new ways to love his grandfather.

What did you notice?

 ## Quotes

"God grant me the serenity to accept the things I cannot change, courage to change the things I can, and wisdom to know the difference."

—THE SERENITY PRAYER, BY REINHOLD NIEBUHR

Next

Check out these other titles:

Crazy Lady!
BY JANE LESLIE CONLY

Dear Mr. Henshaw
BY BEVERLY CLEARY

Frindle
BY ANDREW CLEMENTS

Petey
BY BEN MIKAELSEN

Six Innings
BY JAMES PRELLER

Terpin
BY TOR SEIDLER

The Green Book

Jill Paton Walsh

Story Synopsis

atty and her family and a small group of people leave the dying earth and journey to a new planet. The planet does not seem to be hospitable to them and the adults despair. The children make an important discovery that aids their sustainability, and at the same time, the community redefines what is important to their survival.

Appreciation, community, courage, fairness, greed, ingenuity, interdependence, problem solving, resourcefulness, sustainability, teamwork, tenacity

Who, What, When, and Why

★ Each person is "handpicked" to settle Shine, the new planet. What skills does this new community need? Why are the skills of every single member of the community important?
What skills would you bring to the community?
How resourceful would you be in this situation?

★ What objects brought to Shine prove to be the most useful? What objects prove useless? What makes life on Shine "so deadly"?
Why do stories become so important to the community?

★ What qualities do the children bring to the challenge of surviving on Shine—openness to new ideas, tenacity, courage, teamwork, ingenuity?
Which quality do you think is the most important?
Are these qualities needed for life on earth?

READING TOGETHER

THE
GREEN BOOK
JILL PATON WALSH

Will Pattie and her family survive on the planet Shine?

READ TOGETHER: GRADES 4–5
READ ALONE: GRADE 4+

Souvenir

"We needed some stories to cheer us up."

 Look Closer

☆ **What would you take with you to a new planet?**
What book would you take? What book would be the most useful?
What book would be the most enjoyable?
Which book would you like to read over and over again?

☆ **What would be the hardest thing to tolerate in this situation?**
What would you miss the most from earth?

☆ **Do you take for granted what you have?**
Do you only appreciate something when you don't have it?
What do you value that you have in abundance?

What I Noticed

I was happily surprised that it was the children's common sense, ingenuity, and resourcefulness that helped the community survive.

What did you notice?

 Quotes

"*Sometimes a person needs a story more than food to stay alive.*"
—BARRY LOPEZ

Next

Check out these other titles:

Bound for Oregon
BY JEAN VAN LEEUWEN

Incident at Hawk's Hill
BY ALLAN W. ECKERT

Mrs. Frisby and the Rats of NIMH
BY ROBERT O'BRIEN

The Mysterious Benedict Society
BY TRENTON LEE STEWART

Running Out of Time
BY MARGARET PETERSON HADDIX

The Wonderful Flight to the Mushroom Planet
BY ELEANOR CAMERON

Harriet the Spy

Louise Fitzhugh

WORLD OF IDEAS

Compromise,
friendship, integrity,
knowing the whole story,
little lies,
making amends,
pragmatism,
revenge

Story Synopsis

Harriet wants more than anything to become a famous writer. Ole Golly, her nanny, tells her to observe what is around her and write down what she sees. Harriet carries her notebook with her everywhere and writes about the people in her neighborhood and the students at school. When her notebook is read by her friends, she finds herself an outcast and has to figure out a way to win her friends back.

Who, What, When, and Why

★ What words describe Harriet—*curious, ruthlessly observant, strong willed, clever, a snoop*?
What words describe Ole Golly—*pragmatic, perceptive, wise, well read*?
How would you describe their relationship?
How does Harriet's relationship with Ole Golly differ from her relationship with her parents?

★ Why does Harriet want to be a spy? What does Harriet write in her notebook?

★ Why are Jane and Sport so hurt when they read her observations? Are they lies, observations, opinions, or "truths"?

★ Why do the children read her notebook? Do you think this is right?
Does Harriet write her notebook for anyone else's eyes?
Do you think it is fair for them to build "the spy-catcher club"? Does their revenge feel harsh?

READING TOGETHER

READ TOGETHER: GRADE 4 +

READ ALONE: GRADE 5 +

Souvenir

"But to yourself you must always tell the truth."

Look Closer

☆ If you saw a notebook that said "private," would you read it?
When you read something that is marked "private," does it open Pandora's box?

☆ Many of Harriet's observations didn't take into account that she did not have the whole story. Is there always more to a situation than first meets the eye?

☆ Ole Golly tells Harriet that if someone reads her notebook she is going to have to apologize and lie. Have you ever had to tell a "little lie" to protect a friendship?
Have you ever had to apologize even when you didn't feel sorry?
What makes apologies so difficult?

What I Noticed

I was impressed that Harriet was able to make amends with her friends, knowing full well she was not going to let go of her aspirations to be a famous writer.

What did you notice?

 Quotes

"Tell all the truth but tell it slant."
—EMILY DICKINSON

Next

Check out these other titles:

Because of Winn-Dixie
BY KATE DICAMILLO

Frindle
BY ANDREW CLEMENTS

The Great Gilly Hopkins
BY KATHERINE PATERSON

Love That Dog
BY SHARON CREECH

The School Story
BY ANDREW CLEMENTS

Scooter
BY VERA B. WILLIAMS

Hatchet

Gary Paulsen

WORLD OF IDEAS

Attitude, challenges, courage, fear, hope, life-changing experience, luck, mistakes, resourcefulness, self-reliance, survival skills

Story Synopsis

Brian Robeson is the only passenger on a small plane when the pilot has a heart attack and dies. Brian crashes the plane into a lake and finds himself stranded in the Canadian wilderness with only the clothes he is wearing and the hatchet he received from his mother. With his parents' divorce weighing heavily on his mind, Brian must find the courage, determination, and skills he needs to survive day to day.

Who, What, When, and Why

★ How would you describe Brian at his best—*disciplined, determined to survive, able to learn from his mistakes, a careful thinker, uses common sense*?
How does Brian find food, build a shelter, catch a fish without a fishing pole, start a fire without matches?

★ How would you describe Brian at his worst—*feeling hopeless, feeling sorry for himself, depressed, lonely*?

★ Why doesn't feeling sorry for himself help Brian?
After the search plane comes and goes, Brian says the disappointment cut him down and made him new. What does he mean? How does losing his hope of being rescued change him?
What does he learn about mistakes and laziness in nature?

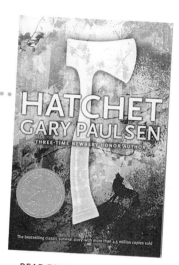

READ TOGETHER: GRADE 5+
READ ALONE: GRADE 6+

 # Look Closer

☆ Have you ever had a life-changing experience?
Does it take a crisis to bring about major changes in a person?

☆ What would be your greatest asset that would help you survive?
What would be your greatest liability?

☆ How would hope, luck, and common sense affect your survival?
Which would be the most important to you?

Souvenir

"That's how Perpich had put it—stay positive and stay on top of things. You are your most valuable asset. Don't forget that. You are the best thing you have."

What I Noticed

I wonder if you only learn about yourself when adversity tests you.

What did you notice?

Next

Check out these other titles:

The Birthday Room
BY KEVIN HENKES

Far North
BY WILL HOBBS

Incident at Hawk's Hill
BY ALLAN W. ECKERT

Island of the Blue Dolphins
BY SCOTT O'DELL

Night of the Twisters
BY IVY RUCKMAN

The Sign of the Beaver
BY ELIZABETH GEORGE SPEARE

 Quotes

"In nature there are neither rewards nor punishments—there are consequences."
—ROBERT G. INGERSOLL

The Jacket

Andrew Clements

False accusation, humiliation, jumping to conclusions, making amends, questioning one's beliefs, prejudice, tolerance

Story Synopsis

After wrongly accusing Daniel of stealing his brother's jacket, Phil is forced to question his beliefs and attitudes about race, class, and prejudice. On a journey from his home to Daniel's home, Phil confronts his preconceived ideas and questions his own beliefs.

Who, What, When, and Why

★ Phil says he was friends with everybody and never paid attention to anybody's color. He asks himself: If Daniel had been white, would he have grabbed him and accused him of stealing the jacket?
   Phil tells Daniel he is sorry, so why can't he "shake the incident from his head"?
   Phil says prejudice means you don't like black people. Is that all it means?

★ Do you think Phil's mom is prejudiced because although she says Lucy is "her friend," she does not go to the movies with her or have her over for dinner like she does with her other friends?

★ Do you think Phil's dad is prejudiced because he says that most sports teams are now mostly black?

★ Phil has already told Daniel he is sorry, but he goes to his house so he can return the jacket. Why does Phil expect Daniel's house to be different from his house?
   Do you think Daniel and Phil will now become friends?

The Jacket

An innocent mistake . . . or something more?

Andrew Clements
Author of the award-winning two-million-copy bestseller FRINDLE

READ TOGETHER: GRADES 4–6
READ ALONE: GRADE 5+

Souvenir

"Being friends with everyone and being someone's friend, those were two different things."

 # Look Closer

☆ **Phil does not consider himself prejudiced but comes to see that it isn't that simple.**
Are *snap judgments, narrow-mindedness, bias, preconceived ideas,* **and** *intolerance* **other words for prejudice?**
Do you think you are prejudiced? What about your friends and family?
Where do people learn prejudice? Are they born prejudiced?
Can you be prejudiced and not know it?
Why do people self-segregate? Does that make them prejudiced?
Can you overcome prejudice? What does it take to overcome a prejudice?

☆ **Are there situations that call for more than an "I'm sorry"?**
If "I'm sorry" isn't enough, what more could you do?

What I Noticed

You have to be careful before you accuse a person, but this story made me realize just how careful you have to be. The consequences of a false accusation are never pretty.

What did you notice?

 ## Quotes

"To carry a grudge is like being stung to death by one bee."
—WILLIAM H. WALTON

 # Next

Check out these other titles:

The Friendship
BY MILDRED D. TAYLOR

Journey to Jo'burg
BY BEVERLEY NAIDOO

The Real Thief
BY WILLIAM STEIG

Song of the Trees
BY MILDRED D. TAYLOR

The Watsons Go to Birmingham—1963
BY CHRISTOPHER PAUL CURTIS

The Lemming Condition

Alan Arkin

WORLD OF IDEAS

Conviction, confusion,
independent thinking,
peer pressure, questioning,
wanting to belong,
weighing consequences

Story Synopsis

Bubber's family and the rest of the lemmings are getting ready for the great march west and the leap into the sea. Bubber is excited until his friend, Crow, starts asking questions— why are you doing this, what comes after the leap, can you even swim? Bubber becomes uncomfortable when he realizes he doesn't know the answers to Crow's questions. These unanswered questions force Bubber to make a tough decision.

Who, What, When, and Why

★ Why do Bubber's parents tell him not to worry?
Why does Arnold tell Bubber not to think too much and just go along with things as they happen?
Why does Uncle Claude tell Bubber he is asking dumb questions?
Are they uncomfortable with Bubbers questions because they don't know the answers?

★ Why does Crow suggest Bubber find out if he can swim?

★ Bubber is conflicted because he doesn't want to be separated from his family and community, but he feels different from the other lemmings and he suspects that they don't know what they're doing. What does the old lemming tell Bubber about lemmings?
Even with his doubts, why does Bubber decide to go along with the march?
Why does he stop himself from following the lemmings at the very end?
Why does he refuse to stay with the surviving lemmings and start over again?

READING TOGETHER

THE LEMMING CONDITION
by Alan Arkin

Illustrated by Joan Sandin

READ TOGETHER: GRADES 4–6
READ ALONE: GRADE 5+

Souvenir

"You didn't think like *you*. You thought like a lemming. You let three loonies make up your mind."

What I Noticed

I was impressed that Bubber chose to leave the lemming community and had the courage to find his place in the world.

What did you notice?

 Quotes

"Do nothing you do not understand."
—PYTHAGORAS

Look Closer

☆ What makes some people comfortable asking questions and other people uncomfortable asking questions? What is your inclination? Why are some people uncomfortable with people who ask questions?
Can you outgrow the habit of asking questions? Would you want to?
Do questions you can't answer make you feel uncomfortable?

☆ Have you ever gone "over the line" and offended a friend by asking him one too many questions? Has someone gone "over the line" with you and asked one too many questions?

☆ Why is it difficult to be an independent thinker?
Can you assume once you are an independent thinker, you will always be an independent thinker?

Next

Check out these other titles:

The Hundred Dresses
BY ELEANOR ESTES

Poppy
BY AVI

Mrs. Frisby and the Rats of NIMH
BY ROBERT O'BRIEN

The Sneetches and Other Stories
BY DR. SEUSS

Love, Ruby Lavender

Deborah Wiles

Accidents, empathy, forgiveness, friendship, grudges, life goes on, reconciliation, grief, self-reliance

Story Synopsis

Ruby Lavender is very close to her grand-mother, Miss Eula, especially since the death of her grandpa. When Miss Eula announces that she is leaving for Hawaii, Ruby feels abandoned and resents that she is stuck in Halleluia, Mississippi, with nothing to do but be tormented by Melba Jane.

Who, What, When, and Why

★ Why does Miss Eula say she needs to go to Hawaii for her and Ruby's sake?
Does Miss Eula think that Ruby needs to become more independent?
Do you think Ruby and Dove would have become friends if Miss Eula hadn't gone to Hawaii?

★ Ruby and Melba Jane are not on good terms after the accident that killed Melba Jane's father and Ruby's grandfather. Why can't Ruby and Melba Jane have empathy for each other's grief?
Why does Melba Jane pretend she is not hurting?
Does Melba Jane hold a grudge against Ruby and blame her for the accident?
Why does Ruby feel responsible for the accident? Is she?

★ What makes Dove a good friend to Ruby? How does she help Ruby get a different perspective on the accident?

★ What happens at the operetta that allows Ruby to have empathy for Melba Jane?
Do you think Melba Jane and Ruby are now going to be good friends?
Does reconciliation automatically mean you will be friends?

Love, Ruby Lavender

Good garden of peas!
What a summer!

DEBORAH WILES

READ TOGETHER: GRADES 4–6
READ ALONE: GRADE 5+

Souvenir

"[Grandpa] told Ruby most people were like lemon drops, sour and sweet together. She couldn't see it."

 # Look Closer

☆ Strong feelings such as sadness and grief are sometimes too painful to face. What do you do when a feeling overwhelms you?
Can you ignore a feeling? Can you ignore a feeling forever?

☆ Is blame an "easier" emotion than sadness? Is blame a good place to hide from your feelings? What purpose does blame serve?

☆ What makes it hard in certain situations to accept forgiveness?
Can you accept forgiveness if you are still blaming someone?
When you don't accept an apology, how do you feel?

☆ How does your perspective change when you "walk in someone else's shoes"?

What I Noticed

I often ask my friends what should I do, but I know most of the time I need to figure it out for myself.

What did you notice?

 Quotes

"There ain't no cloud so thick that the sun ain't shinin' on t'other side."
—RATTLESNAKE, AN 1870S MOUNTAIN MAN

Next

Check out these other titles:

All Alone in the Universe
BY LYNNE RAE PERKINS

Clementine
BY SARA PENNYPACKER

Harriet the Spy
BY LOUISE FITZHUGH

Missing May
BY CYNTHIA RYLANT

My Louisiana Sky
BY KIMBERLY WILLIS HOLT

The Trouble with Cats
BY MARTHA FREEMAN

The Most Beautiful Place in the World

Ann Cameron

WORLD OF IDEAS

Challenges, expectations,
love, perseverance,
poverty, pragmatism,
sticking up for yourself

Story Synopsis

Juan lives on the shores of Lake Atitlán in Guatemala amid beautiful fields and flocks of colorful parrots. Although surrounded by such beauty, Juan lives in poverty, abandoned by his mother and living with his grandmother. Juan's difficult life is balanced by his grandmother's wisdom that the most beautiful place in the world is "anyplace you can hold your head up."

Who, What, When, and Why

★ Why does Juan think his grandmother doesn't want to send him to school? What makes Juan finally decide to ask his grandmother if he can go to school?
Why does Juan tell himself school doesn't really matter?
Have you ever told yourself something doesn't matter when you know it does?

★ Juan's grandmother tells him when something is important, you've got to say it—you have to stand up for yourself. Why does his grandmother not accept Doña Irene's answer that Juan can start school but not until next year?

★ Juan says that doing his best all the time can get pretty inconvenient. Why does Juan's grandmother insist that he do his best all the time?
Do you think his grandmother expects too much from him?
Is she being harsh or is she being pragmatic, given the situation?
Does she love him more than anyone else?

ANN CAMERON

The Most Beautiful Place in the World

YEARLING

drawings by
THOMAS B. ALLEN

READ TOGETHER: GRADES 3–5
READ ALONE: GRADE 4+

Souvenir

"'You ask more from me than Doña Irene and all the teachers,' I said. 'They don't expect so much.' My grandmother glared at me. 'They don't love you the way I do either,' she said."

 ## Look Closer

☆ What is the most beautiful place in the world to you? What makes it beautiful?

☆ Why is sticking up for yourself so important and sometimes so difficult?

☆ Can someone love somebody and not have expectations?
Are expectations a burden or a gift?
What happens when you expect too little?
What happens when you expect too much?

☆ Do you expect to do your best all the time?
Is it important to do your best in all situations, or just in important situations?

☆ The story is both happy and sad. When the story ends, how do you feel?

What I Noticed

I really liked the grandmother's advice: Always stand up for what is important to you.

What did you notice?

Quotes

"Be like a postage stamp. Stick to one thing until you get there."
—JOSH BILLINGS

Next

Check out these other titles:

Beatrice's Goat
BY PAGE MCBRIER

A Horn for Louis
BY ERIC KIMMEL

Rickshaw Girl
BY MITALI PERKINS

The School Mouse
BY DICK KING-SMITH

The Year of Miss Agnes
BY KIRKPATRICK HILL

Mrs. Frisby and the Rats of NIMH

Robert O'Brien

WORLD OF IDEAS

Courage, determination, loyalty, overcoming fears, problem solving, risks, self-sufficiency, the responsibility of intelligence, tough choices

Story Synopsis

Mrs. Frisby, a widowed mouse with four young children, seeks the help from the Rats of NIMH when her youngest son falls ill and cannot be moved from their winter home. The Rats of NIMH, a breed of highly intelligent rodents, not only come up with a solution to her dilemma but also come to fulfill their dream of living a self-sufficient life.

Who, What, When, and Why

★ What are some of the risks and challenges Mrs. Frisby faces in looking for the solution to her problem?

★ With all of the "advantages" in the lab—the rats were "treated well," fed, and kept safe from predators—what bothers them about their captivity? How does their intelligence make it difficult for the rats to live by stealing?

★ Why do the rats decide to leave the Boniface estate? Does life become too easy?
Why is it important for the rats to move to Thorn Valley? What is their plan?

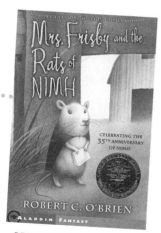

READ-TOGETHER: GRADE 4+
READ ALONE: GRADE 5+

Souvenir

"We're just living on the edge of some-body else's [civilization] like fleas on a dog's back. If the dog drowns, the fleas drown too."

 # Look Closer

☆ Moving to Thorn Valley means the rats have to establish a new way of life and be self-sufficient. Would you be willing and eager to move to Thorn Valley? Why or why not? What traits would you need to be successful in Thorn Valley?

☆ The intentions to use rats for experimentation are good—trying to find cures for disease—but do the intentions justify the means?
If not, what solution would you suggest to replace using animals to better understand health and disease?

☆ Does an easy life prepare you to thrive on your own?
Can you learn to live on your own if everything is done for you?

What I Noticed

This story reminds me of something my parents always say: One generation plants the trees and another gets the shade.

What did you notice?

 Quotes

"'Brick walls are there for a reason,' he told his audience at Carnegie Mellon. 'They let us prove how badly we want things.'"
—*THE LAST LECTURE*, BY RANDY PAUSCH

Next

Check out these other titles:

The Green Book
BY JILL PATON WALSH

Kildee House
BY RUTHERFORD G. MONTGOMERY

The Lemming Condition
BY ALAN ARKIN

Perloo the Bold
BY AVI

Rabbit Hill
BY ROBERT LAWSON

Time Stops for No Mouse
BY MICHAEL HOYE

The Mysterious Benedict Society

Trenton Lee Stewart

Story Synopsis

Four gifted children are recruited by Mr. Benedict to go undercover and find out the intentions of the Learning Institute for the Very Enlightened. Each child has a special talent, which makes each one important to the mission. Through teamwork and wit the children are challenged to uncover the sinister plan of Mr. Curtain's Learning Institute and are able to solve the mystery.

Who, What, When, and Why

★ What special talents and abilities do Reynie, Kate, Sticky, and Constance use to defeat Mr. Curtain's scheme to take over the world?
Why does Mr. Benedict think that only a team of children, working together, can succeed in finding the purpose of the Learning Institute for the Very Enlightened?

★ What is the mission of the Learning Institute for the Very Enlightened?
How does the whisperer machine work?
How does "brainsweeping" make it easy for Mr. Curtain's scheme to work?

Trenton Lee Stewart

READ TOGETHER: GRADE 4+
READ ALONE: GRADE 5+

Souvenir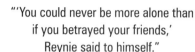

"'You could never be more alone than
if you betrayed your friends,'
Reynie said to himself."

What I Noticed

I loved the way each character had his
own unique approach to solving a
problem.

What did you notice?

 Quotes

*"I never doubt that a small group of thoughtful,
committed citizens can change the world.
Indeed, it is the only thing that ever has."*

—MARGARET MEAD

 # Look Closer

☆ Mr. Curtain believes that if he can "remove"
peoples' fears they will be happy and easier
to control. Why do you think fear is such a
powerful emotion?

☆ Is there a point in the story when you think
you would have given up?
What would be your greatest strength and what
would be your greatest liability? Are you stubborn like Constance? Do you think you are
invincible like Kate?

☆ By using subliminal messages, the whisperer
promotes peoples' happiness by getting them
to forget their fears. What makes it hard to
resist an idea that comes in below the thresh-
old of consciousness?
Do commercials and advertisements work the
same as the whisperer?

Next

Check out these other titles:

Chasing Vermeer
BY BLUE BALLIETT (6+)

The Star of Kazan
BY EVA IBBOTSON

The Thief Lord
BY CORNELIA FUNKE

The View from Saturday
BY E. L. KONIGSBURG

*The Wonderful Flight
to the Mushroom Planet*
BY ELEANOR CAMERON

Notes from a Liar and Her Dog

Gennifer Choldenko

Bravado, consequences, facing your feelings, family dynamics, favoritism in a family, feeling misunderstood, justifying lies, mistakes, perspective, trust

Story Synopsis

Ant feels like she was "misplaced at birth"— she is the opposite of her two "perfect" sisters and feels her mother doesn't understand her. She takes solace in creating a fantasy family and writing in her journal to her "real" mother. Ant's art teacher steps in and tries to help when she detects Ant's unhappiness and becomes aware of her constant lying.

Who, What, When, and Why

★ **Why does Ant pretend she is adopted?**
Why does Ant feel misunderstood by her family?
Why does Ant lie? Why do her "little green lies" make her feel safe?
Why does Ant say lies are the only way she can handle her mom?

★ **"Just Carol," the young new art teacher, sees beyond Ant's bravado, her "I don't care" attitude. Why does "Just Carol" insist that Ant stop justifying her lies?**
Why is it hard for Ant to stop lying? Why is it hard for her to tell her mom about the vet bill?

★ **Ant feels constantly criticized by her mother who she thinks doesn't love her. How does knowing her mom "tried to be a good mom" help Ant accept her?**
What changes for Ant when she sees things from her mother's perspective?
How do Ant's feelings change after her mom apologizes?
What does it mean when Ant's mom agrees to call her Ant and not Antonia?

READ TOGETHER: GRADE 5+
READ ALONE: GRADE 6+

 **Look Closer**

☆ Do you feel there are favorites in your family? How can parents play favorites? Do you need to understand and accept a person to love them?

☆ What makes it difficult to trust a person who lies?
Is there always a reason why a person lies? Is it important to know the reason?

☆ Are *bragging, courageous, blustering, boasting, pretentious,* and *swagger* other words for **bravado**?

 Souvenir

"Before Harrison, I had people I called friends, but they were just kids to eat lunch with. That's way different."

What I Noticed

I wonder how the story would have been different if it had been told from the mom's perspective.

What did you notice?

 Quotes

"If you do not tell the truth about yourself you cannot tell it about other people."
—VIRGINIA WOOLF

Next

Check out these other titles:

Dear Mr. Henshaw
BY BEVERLY CLEARY

Dovey Coe
BY FRANCES O'ROARK DOWELL

The Great Gilly Hopkins
BY KATHERINE PATERSON

Harriet the Spy
BY LOUISE FITZHUGH

Love, Ruby Lavender
BY DEBORAH WILES

The Other Side of Silence
BY MARGARET MAHY (6+)

On My Honor

Marion Dane Bauer

WORLD OF IDEAS

Accidents, blame, choices, consequences, dares, death, fear, guilt, life-changing experience, peer pressure, regret, taunts

Story Synopsis

Tony and Joel have been friends since they were little. When Tony and Joel ride their bikes out to the cliffs at Starved Rock, Tony dares Joel to a race across the Vermillion River. The river is dangerous and when Joel finally makes it to the other side, he turns to look for Tony but finds that he has vanished.

Who, What, When, and Why

★ Tony and Joel are very different. Why are they such good friends? Why does Tony make "empty" boasts?

★ Why does Tony taunt Joel? Is he trying to show off? Is he trying to cover up his own fears and insecurities?
Why does Joel start taunting Tony?

★ Joel promises to report Tony's drowning to the police, but doesn't. Why does he make up a story about what happened? Does he think the police will blame him for Tony's accident? Does he think he caused Tony's accident?

★ Whose fault, do you think, is Tony's death—Joel, Joel's dad, or Tony? Why does Joel want to find someone to blame? Can blame keep him from feeling the sadness of losing Tony?

READING TOGETHER

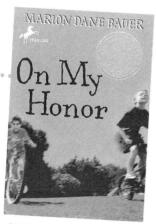

MARION DANE BAUER

On My Honor

READ TOGETHER: GRADE 5+
READ ALONE: GRADE 6+

 # Look Closer

☆ Do you sometimes "need" your parents to give you limits so that you can use the fall-back line, "My parents said no"?

☆ What is the difference between a taunt (mock, ridicule, tease) and a dare (challenge, insult, provocation)?
What happens when you taunt someone? What are the results? Is it ever smart to taunt someone?

☆ Do you have friends like Tony who like to do "crazy things" and talk you into doing things you really don't want to do?

Souvenir

"You can't live your life by maybes."

What I Noticed

The story made me understand that if I go along with what a friend does, I have some responsibility for what happens.

What did you notice?

 # Next

Check out these other titles:

Bridge to Terabithia
BY KATHERINE PATERSON

Hatchet
BY GARY PAULSEN

Love, Ruby Lavender
BY DEBORAH WILES

Tuck Everlasting
BY NATALIE BABBITT

 # Quotes

"Every heart hath its own ache."
—THOMAS FULLER

Petey

Ben Mikaelsen

Attitude, bullies,
disabilities, empathy,
hope, indifference,
making a difference,
unlikely friendships

Story Synopsis

Walking home one day from school, Trevor Ladd, a new student, catches some bullies throwing snowballs at Petey, an old man in a nursing home. This deed leads to an unlikely friendship with Petey, who has cerebral palsy and has lived in institutions all his life. Trevor finds his life transformed as he gets to know Petey and learns about the strength of the human spirit.

Who, What, When, and Why

★ How do Esteban, Joe, Cassie, Owen, Sissy, and Calvin make a difference in Petey's life?
How does Petey make a difference in their lives?
What does Trevor mean when he says Petey is good for everyone?

★ Why does Trevor change his mind and become Petey's friend?
How do they each make a difference in each other's lives?

★ Why is Petey able to be happy? Are you born with a capacity for happiness?

READ TOGETHER: GRADE 5+
READ ALONE: GRADE 6+

 Souvenir

"A jewel is just a rock that figured out
how to shine."

 Look Closer

☆ Are you born with the desire to be involved? Why do some people get involved and others remain indifferent? How does having empathy and compassion for a person make it difficult to remain indifferent?

☆ How do we learn to see beyond surface appearances?

☆ How would your parents react to your friendship with someone like Petey?

☆ Petey asks himself what his purpose is in life. What is yours?
Is anyone in the world better off because you exist?

 What I Noticed

I would like to think I am the person at the Kmart who smiled and said hello to Petey.

What did you notice?

 Next

Check out these other titles:

Crazy Lady!
BY JANE LESLIE CONLY

Holes
BY LOUIS SACHAR

Orphan Train Rider
BY ANDREA WARREN

Rules
BY CYNTHIA LORD

The Young Man and the Sea
BY RODMAN PHILBRICK

 **Quotes**

*"No act of kindness, no matter how small,
is ever wasted."*

—AESOP

Poppy

Avi

WORLD OF IDEAS

Bravery, bullies,
cockiness, courage,
fears, flattery,
independent thinking,
intimidation, phoniness,
taunts, tyranny

Story Synopsis

Poppy lives with her large family in an abandoned farmhouse. They are ruled over by the sinister Mr. Ocax, an owl, who promises them protection as long as they obey him. Poppy is a sweet and obedient daughter until she witnesses Ocax kill and eat her boyfriend, Ragweed. Poppy finds her way from cowardice to courage when she sets out on a quest to find her family a new home and prove to them that Mr. Ocax is a phony.

Who, What, When, and Why

★ **Why do the other mice dislike Ragweed? What words describe Ragweed—** *thoughtless, headstrong, disrespectful, cocky, independent*?
Ragweed is curious and persistent. What bothers the other mice about his questions? Is he too much of an independent thinker?

★ **What gives Poppy the courage to undertake the dangerous journey to New House? Is she inspired by Ragweed's independent thinking?**
Does she feel unjustly blamed by the community? Does she feel responsible for the well-being of the community?
When does Poppy begin to suspect that Mr. Ocax is a phony?
Why is it a mistake to taunt Mr. Ocax?

★ **What words describe Mr. Ocax—***liar, phony, bully, intimidating, tyrant, coward*?
Whose best interests is Mr. Ocax protecting?
How does he intimidate the mice and prey on their fears and ignorance?

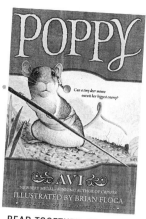

READ TOGETHER: GRADE 4+
READ ALONE: GRADE 5+

Souvenir

"'Ragweed,' she persisted even as she began to creep into the open, 'being careless is stupid.'"

 Look Closer

☆ How does intimidation work? Have you ever felt intimidated by someone?

☆ Poppy says it is hard to be courageous and hard to be a coward—it's easier just to do nothing. What is more difficult, being courageous or being a coward? What makes "doing the right thing" so difficult?

☆ Lungwort says he does not want flattery but needs hard criticism. What is more useful, flattery or criticism? Why are both so important?

☆ What happens when you taunt someone? What are the results? Is it ever smart to taunt someone?

What I Noticed

I was surprised that Poppy allowed herself to be flattered by Mr. Ocax, and I realized how flattery can cloud your thinking.

What did you notice?

Next

Check out these other titles:

The Lemming Condition
BY ALAN ARKIN

On My Honor
BY MARION DANE BAUER

Rabbit Hill
BY ROBERT LAWSON

The Search for Delicious
BY NATALIE BABBITT

Stuart Little
BY E. B. WHITE

The Tale of Despereaux
BY KATE DICAMILLO

Quotes

"You've got to be able to make those daring leaps or you're nowhere."
—RUSSELL HOBAN

The Search for Delicious

Natalie Babbitt

Good versus evil, gullibility, ideals, indifference, making a difference, manipulation, motives, responsibility of leadership, rumors, wordplay

Story Synopsis

When the king orders the prime minister to write a dictionary, a dispute erupts over the meaning of the word *delicious*. Gaylen, the prime minister's son, is sent to the countryside to take a poll on what the word *delicious* means. Chaos erupts because no two definitions are the same. In this time of turmoil, Gaylen finds the kingdom in jeopardy due to Hemlock's evil plan to start a civil war.

Who, What, When, and Why

★ What does Gaylen discover on his journey? Why does Gaylen go from wanting to help the king to not wanting to even live among people? What annoys him about their behavior?
Why does Gaylen change his mind and decide to go back and try to save the kingdom from Hemlocks' evil plan?

★ How does Hemlock turn the people against the king? How does he use the search for the definition of the word *delicious* to his advantage?
Why are the people so willing to believe Hemlock's lies about the king?
Why do the people believe Hemlock is on the side of good? Does he give the people any reasons to think he might be a better ruler than the king?

READ TOGETHER: GRADES 3–5

READ ALONE: GRADE 4+

Souvenir

"He looked up at the trees and sighed, 'It's easy for you to stand there all along. You don't know how it feels to care about anything. Why, you don't even care about not caring!'"

 Look Closer

☆ Why are people sometimes so easily fooled? How gullible are you? How trusting are you?

☆ Hemlock is a friend to no one. What makes that kind of person dangerous?

☆ Hemlock's actions are motivated by his wish to gain personal power whereas Gaylen's actions are motivated by his caring for the greater good of the kingdom. Do you need to understand someone's motives to know their true intention?

☆ What is your definition of *delicious*? Does your definition of *delicious* constantly change?

What I Noticed

Hemlock showed me knocking something down is easier than building something up.

What did you notice?

 **Quotes**

"*You ain't got nothing to back you up 'cept what you got in your heart.*"

—*SCORPIONS*, WALTER DEAN MYERS

Next

Check out these other titles:

Gawgon and the Boy
BY LLOYD ALEXANDER

King Matt the First
BY JANUSZ KORCZAK (6+)

The Little Prince
BY ANTOINE DE SAINT-EXUPERY

A String in the Harp
BY NANCY BOND (6+)

The Waterstone
BY REBECCA RUPP

The Wonderful O
BY JAMES THURBER

Shredderman: Secret Identity

Wendelin Van Draanen

Story Synopsis

Fifth-grader Nolan Byrd, tied of being called names by Bubba, the class bully, creates a "cyber-superhero"— Shredderman. This secret identity changes his life as he sets out to free himself from Bubba's relentless tormenting.

Who, What, When, and Why

★ Why does Nolan, nicknamed NERD by Bubba, allow himself to be bullied by Bubba?
   What does Nolan do, or not do, that sets himself up to be bullied?
   What happens when he confronts the name-calling and the shoving?

★ Nolan is fed up with being bullied and comes up with a plan to expose Bubba's bullying by catching him in the act with a secret camera. How does having a plan change Nolan's attitude and behavior?

★ How does Mr. Green telling Nolan, "You shred, man! Awesome!" change Nolan's feelings about himself? Why does Nolan's secret identity give him a new outlook?

★ At the end of the story Bubba is still a bully but he can't bully Nolan. What's changed about Nolan that makes it impossible for Bubba to bully him?
   Why does Nolan decide to write his report on his dad?

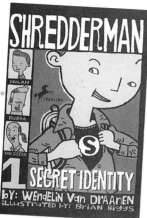

READ TOGETHER: GRADES 3–5
READ ALONE: GRADE 4+

Souvenir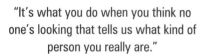

"It's what you do when you think no one's looking that tells us what kind of person you really are."

What I Noticed

I never stopped to ask myself why a person becomes a bully, and how unhappy they must be.

What did you notice?

Quotes

"When we are no longer able to change a situation, we are challenged to change ourselves."

—VICTOR FRANKL

 ## Look Closer

☆ Bullies are never going to disappear but one of the ways you can protect yourself is to understand what makes them tick. Have you ever met a happy bully?
Why does a person become a bully?
How does the way you respond to a bully become part of the problem? How could your behavior be part of the remedy?
How easy is it to bully an individual versus a crowd?

☆ Does how you see yourself influence how people see you? What image do you project to your friends?
Can you project an image that is false?

☆ Where do you learn to stick up for yourself? What makes it difficult?

☆ What happens when you don't stick up for yourself?

☆ The school principal says bullies help you get ready for life. Do you agree?

Next

Check out these other titles:

Diary of a Wimpy Kid
BY JEFF KINNEY

The Homework Machine
BY DAN GUTMAN

Loser
BY JERRY SPINELLI

Owen Foote, Soccer Star
BY STEPHANIE GREENE

A Single Shard

Linda Sue Park

WORLD OF IDEAS

Adventure, courage, creativity, family, gratitude, innovation, opportunity, perfection, perseverance, pride, promises, resourcefulness, shame, fear

Story Synopsis

Tree-ear, an orphan in a twelfth-century Korean potter's village, lives under the bridge with the crippled and homeless Crane-man. When Tree-ear accidentally breaks a pot at the famous master Min's studio, he pays his debt in servitude. Forced to make a perilous journey, Tree-ear overcomes difficult situations that both challenge and test his courage.

Who, What, When, and Why

★ Even though Tree-ear and Crane-man are not related by blood, they function as father and son. What words describe their relationship—*protective, kind, devoted, loving, caring, supportive*?
How do they show their care and affection for each other?

★ What kind of reputation does Min have as a potter? What makes his work superior to Kang's?
Why does Tree-ear think Min has too much pride? Do you agree?
Is Min too much of a perfectionist? Can a perfectionist ever be satisfied?
Are you a perfectionist? Can you be a perfectionist in some areas and not in others?

★ Why is Min reluctant to take Tree-ear on as an assistant? What does Tree-ear do to earn Min's trust?
Tree-ear gets an apprenticeship, a family, and a home from Ajima and Min. What do they get from him?

READING TOGETHER

A SINGLE SHARD
Linda Sue Park

READ TOGETHER: GRADE 5+
READ ALONE: GRADE 6+

Souvenir

"'My friend, the same wind that blows one door shut often blows another open,' he said."

 ## Look Closer

☆ When Tree-ear has no money for the bandits, the bandits decide to have a "little fun." What bothers you about the bandits having a little fun? What is so disturbing about senseless destruction or vandalism?

☆ Crane-man asks Tree-ear, "Is it stealing to take from another something that cannot be held in your hands?" Can you own a creative idea?

☆ Do you believe that if you say you are going to do something, you have to do it?

☆ In Tree-ear's culture, people greet each other with "Have you eaten well today?" If you could make up a greeting, other than "Hi, how are you?" what would it be?

 ### What I Noticed

I loved how Ajima asked Crane-man to help her while Tree-ear was away, which allowed him to save face and keep his dignity.

What did you notice?

 ### Next

Check out these other titles:

The Conch Bearer
BY CHITRA BANERJEE DIVAKARUNI

Crow and Weasel
BY BARRY LOPEZ

The Crow-Girl
BY BODIL BREDSDORFF

Silk Umbrellas
BY CAROLYN MARSDEN

 ## Quotes

"No great thing is created suddenly."
—EPICTETUS

Six Innings

James Preller

WORLD OF IDEAS

Acceptance,
friendship, illness,
Little League baseball,
passion, siblings,
teamwork,
vulnerability

Story Synopsis

Sam and Mike are best friends and love to play baseball, but their friendship is challenged when Sam is diagnosed with cancer and can no longer play. Their story, along with the twenty-four other players, is told, inning by inning and pitch by pitch, against the backdrop of the biggest game of their lives—the Little League National Championship.

Who, What, When, and Why

★ Why don't Sam and Mike talk about their friendship? Does Sam think Mike feels sorry for him? Does he think Mike can't understand?
At the end of the story, what does Sam come to understand about Mike's friendship?

★ What makes the position of pitcher difficult? Would you ever want to pitch?
Do you think the position of pitcher is the most responsible position of the team? What position do you think is the most responsible for the game's outcome?
Is there any position that is not important to the game?

★ At the end of the game, why does Sam sympathize with Nick Clemente? How does he know how he feels?

READING TOGETHER

READ TOGETHER: GRADE 5+
READ ALONE: GRADE 6+

Souvenir

"Sam was the voice over the loudspeaker, the storyteller, the soul of the game."

What I Noticed

Although Sam couldn't play on the field anymore, I admire his attitude and passion to be part of the game in whatever way was possible.

What did you notice?

 **Quotes**

"My whole philosophy is to broadcast the way a fan would broadcast."
—HARRY CARAY

 # Look Closer

☆ What position would you like to play in baseball? Is there a position you would like to play but don't feel you would be good enough?
Would you want your father to be the coach?

☆ Sam says that no one knows how he feels. Can you understand something you have not experienced?
If you had a friend going though a serious illness, what do you think they would need from you?

☆ Carter tells us he keeps his "sense of un-ease" hidden from his friends. Are there things you are not willing to share with your friends? Why?
What makes it hard to share your vulnera-bilities?

 # Next

Check out these other titles:

The Big Field
BY MIKE LUPICA (6+)

Finding Buck McHenry
BY ALFRED SLOTE

The Boy Who Saved Baseball
BY JOHN. H. RITTER (6+)

The Kid Who Only Hit Homers
BY MATT CHRISTOPHER

Keeping Score
BY LINDA SUE PARK (6+)

Shakespeare Bats Cleanup
BY RON KOERTGE (6+)

The Story of a Seagull and the Cat Who Taught Her to Fly

Luis Sepúlveda

WORLD OF IDEAS

Courage,
finding your destiny,
overcoming fear,
promises, risks,
self-confidence, tolerance,
trust, unlikely friendships

Story Synopsis

A seagull, dying from the effects of an oil spill, entrusts her egg to Zorba, the cat, who promises to watch over her egg, not to eat the chick when it hatches, and to teach the baby gull to fly. Teaching the baby chick to fly and helping the chick realize her true nature proves more complicated than Zorba anticipated, and he finds himself challenged in ways he didn't expect.

Who, What, When, and Why

★ What does the mother seagull ask Zorba to promise?
Why does he agree to such a "generous" promise? Does he have a choice? What part of the promise is difficult for Zorba to keep?

★ Why does the baby gull call Zorba her mommy and say he is a very good mommy? Why doesn't Zorba just adopt the gull chick and raise her as his own?

★ Lucky tells Zorba she doesn't want to be a seagull and fly, she wants to be a cat. What does Zorba mean when he tells Lucky she must follow her destiny as a seagull?
Why does Zorba tell Lucky she will be happy when she follows her destiny? Why does Lucky spread her wings when she sees gulls flying? Is it instinct?

★ The poet doesn't know how to fly with bird's wings but Zorba says he makes him feel like he's flying with his words. Is this why Zorba chooses the poet to teach Lucky to fly? How does the poet teach Lucky to fly?

★ Why is Zorba crying at the end of the story? Is this a sad story?

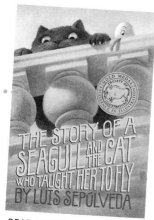

READ TOGETHER: GRADES 3–5

READ ALONE: GRADE 4+

Souvenir

"It's very easy to accept and love those who are like us, but to love someone different is very hard, and you have helped us do that."

 # Look Closer

☆ A person makes a promise with the best of intentions. Do you think it is okay to keep only part of a promise?

Which is more difficult, keeping a promise to yourself or to another person?

☆ What is the difference between an honor code and a promise? Is an honor code the promises a person makes to himself or herself?

☆ Could you substitute the words *fortune* and *fate* for *destiny*?

What does it mean to follow your destiny?

☆ Lucky was reluctant to take the risk to see if she could fly. What do you need to take risks—courage, faith in yourself, nerve, self-confidence, or no fear of failing?

Are you a risk taker? What makes taking risks difficult?

If you don't take risks, what can you accomplish?

What I Noticed

Make sure you can keep a promise before you make a promise.

What did you notice?

 ## Quotes

"Well done is better than well said."
—BENJAMIN FRANKLIN

 ## Next

Check out these other titles:

Charlotte's Web
BY E. B. WHITE

The Land of Green Ginger
BY NOEL LANGLEY

The Music of Dolphins
BY KAREN HESSE

A Single Shard
BY LINDA SUE PARK

The Tale of Despereaux
BY KATE DICAMILLO

The Trumpet of the Swan

E. B. White

WORLD OF IDEAS

Attitude, being different, disability, end justifies the means, freedom, love, overcoming obstacles, pragmatism, promises, resourcefulness

Story Synopsis

Louis, a trumpeter swan, is born without a voice and desperately wants to find a way to communicate. His friend Sam helps him learn to read and write so he can communicate but none of the other swans can understand him. Finally, Louis gets a voice when his father, the cob, steals a trumpet from a music store. Louis's adventure begins as he flies across the United States working and performing to pay back the money owed for the stolen trumpet.

Who, What, When, and Why

★ What words describe Louis—*pragmatic, resourceful, determined, hardworking, honorable*?

★ The cob stole the trumpet for the love of his son. How does the cob feel about stealing the trumpet?
Do you think it was the right thing to do?
Why is Louis so determined to pay for his trumpet?

★ What bothers Louis and Serena about the offer for both of them to live at the zoo, where they will be safe and well taken care of?
Why is it so important for Louis to live in a wild place?
What solution does Sam help Louis figure out?

★ In what ways does Louis help Sam?

READING TOGETHER

READ TOGETHER: GRADES 3–5
READ ALONE: GRADE 4+

 ## Look Closer

☆ If you could not speak what other ways would you find to communicate?

☆ Is there ever a situation which justifies stealing?

☆ Louis feels overloaded with stuff around his neck. Do you like having a lot of stuff?
Does stuff bog you down? Do you have too much stuff? Do you need all of your stuff? Where do you get money to buy your stuff?

 ## Souvenir

"Louis is following a dream. We must all follow a dream."

 ## What I Noticed

I loved that Louis worked hard to pay for the stolen trumpet.

What did you notice?

Next

Check out these other titles:

A Bear Named Trouble
BY MARION DANE BAUER

The Monster Garden
BY VIVIEN ALCOCK

Mrs. Frisby and the Rats of NIMH
BY ROBERT O'BRIEN

Poppy
BY AVI

The Story of a Seagull and the Cat Who Taught Her to Fly
BY LUIS SEPÚLVEDA

 ## Quotes

"Necessity is the mother of taking chances."
—MARK TWAIN

Tuck Everlasting

Natalie Babbitt

WORLD OF IDEAS

Choices, consequences,
cycle of life,
individual sense of
right and wrong,
immortality,
making a difference, murder

Story Synopsis

One day Winnie Foster sneaks off into the wood and comes upon a spring where she meets the Tuck family and the secret they've sworn to protect: a hidden spring that grants immortality to anyone who drinks the water. Both Winnie and the Tuck family are confronted with an agonizing situation when they discover that a malicious stranger knows about their secret.

Who, What, When, and Why

★ The Tuck family—Tuck, Mae, Miles, and Jesse—each feel differently about their immortality. What makes Jesse able to easily accept their situation?
Why does Miles feel responsible to do something useful in the world?
Why does Mae call their immortality a curse?
What bothers Tuck about how things stay the same and never change?
In what ways does Tuck's explanation about the spring change Winnie's perspective?

★ Why does the man in the yellow suit want to own the wood?
What makes his plan so sinister? Why is the spring a dangerous secret?
Why does Mae shoot the man in the yellow suit? What is she trying to prevent him from doing?

★ What makes Winnie decide to help the Tucks rescue Mae? Was it their friendship, her sense of rightness, or her desire to make a difference in the world?

READ TOGETHER: GRADES 4–6
READ ALONE: GRADE 5+

Souvenir

"But dying's part of the wheel, right there next to being born. You can't pick out the pieces you like and leave the rest. Being part of the whole thing, that's the blessing."

 Look Closer

☆ Things staying the same, nothing ever changing, living forever—would you choose immortality?
What would be the benefits of immortality? What would be the drawbacks of immortality?
Are you surprised that Winnie did not drink from the spring? Did you want her to drink from the spring?

☆ Do you think Mae was justified in shooting the man in the yellow suit?
Where do you get your sense of right and wrong?

What I Noticed

I found it interesting that each member of the Tuck family had such different feelings about their immortality.

What did you notice?

 **Quotes**

"You don't get to choose how you're going to die. Or when. You can only decide how you're going to live."
—JOAN BAEZ

Next

Check out these other titles:

Dovey Coe
BY FRANCES O'ROARK DOWELL

The Giver
BY LOIS LOWRY (6+)

Mrs. Frisby and the Rats of NIMH
BY ROBERT O'BRIEN

Petey
BY BEN MIKAELSEN

The Story of a Seagull and the Cat Who Taught Her to Fly
BY LUIS SEPÚLVEDA

Two Old Women

Velma Wallis

Being productive,
betrayal, community,
complaining, hardship,
leadership, pragmatism,
resourcefulness,
survival, thriving, trust

Story Synopsis

An Athabascan Indian tale of two old women who are abandoned by their tribe at a time of famine. The two decide not to passively wait for death but to figure out a way to survive. In rediscovering the skills of their youth, they find strength, wisdom, friendship, and eventually are able to forgive the community for their harsh decision to abandon them.

Who, What, When, and Why

★ In this culture everyone has a responsibility to ensure the community's survival. Why does the community go along with the chief's decision to leave the old women behind?

What are the pragmatic rules this community lives by?

Why, at the end of the story, does the chief change his mind? Is his change of mind a sign of weakness as a leader or a sign of strength?

★ What makes the two old women unproductive? What makes their complaining such a serious problem?

What are their vulnerabilities?

What skills help them survive?

Why do they lose their trust in people and become fearful of them?

★ How does the women's return affect the community?

What do the two old women come to value after their experience?

READING TOGETHER

READ TOGETHER: GRADE 5+
READ ALONE: GRADE 6+

Souvenir

"Stories are gifts given by an elder to a younger person."

 **Look Closer**

☆ How do stories about your past help you understand who you are? What stories do you have from your family history? Do you have a favorite family story? What story would you choose to hand down to your children?

☆ Is complaining a habit? Where does complaining get you?

☆ What makes you respect a person, their accomplishments or their struggles?

☆ Can you understand a culture that operates on different rules from your own? Is everything relative? Are there "rights" and "wrongs" that apply to all cultures? What about cannibalism?

What I Noticed

These two old women made me realize that no matter how old I become I never want to feel that I am finished with doing my share in life.

What did you notice?

 **Quotes**

"When you cease to make a contribution you begin to die."
—ELEANOR ROOSEVELT

 Next

Check out these other titles:

The Haymeadow
BY GARY PAULSEN

Incident at Hawk's Hill
BY ALLAN W. ECKERT

Island of the Blue Dolphins
BY SCOTT O'DELL

Maroo of the Winter Caves
BY ANN TURNBULL

The Sign of the Beaver
BY ELIZABETH GEORGE SPEARE

The Wonderful Flight to the Mushroom Planet

Eleanor Cameron

WORLD OF IDEAS

Adventure, belief, courage, creative thinking, doubt, imagination, passion, willingness to believe

Story Synopsis

Chuck and David answer a newspaper ad from Mr. Bass, a mysterious man who inspires the two boys to build a spaceship, travel to the planet of Basidium, and help the mushroom people. Their determination to save the tiny mushroom planet from a terrible fate challenges them to think in new ways.

Who, What, When, and Why

★ Why is David the right boy for this adventure?
Who would you choose to be your companion on an adventure?

★ Why does Mr. Bass only want children and not adults for his adventure?
Why does he say doubt will ruin things? Who do you think doubts more, children or adults?
Why do you think David and Chuck are able to understand the mushroom people? Is it because they believe in their existence?

★ Why are David and Chuck able to solve the mystery about what is making the mushroom people sick, whereas Mebe and Oru, the wisemen, cannot?
How does "experimenting" with your thinking and using common sense affect an outcome?
How does Mrs. Pennyfeather become the solution to keeping the mushroom people healthy?

★ What would change for the Basidiumites if David and Chuck took visitors there?

ELEANOR CAMERON
THE WONDERFUL FLIGHT TO THE MUSHROOM PLANET

READ TOGETHER: GRADES 4–6
READ ALONE: GRADE 5+

Souvenir

"You boys wasted no time in doubting."

 Look Closer

☆ Does doubt take good energy away from what you have to do? Is it a waste of time and energy?
Does doubt ever serve a good purpose? Does it ever force you to reconsider? Is your natural inclination to doubt?

☆ How creative a thinker are you? How willing are you to "experiment" with your thinking? Who is the most creative thinker you know? What makes that person a creative thinker?

☆ Do the adults in this story believe David and Chuck? Do you? Do you want to? Do you think people lose the capacity to believe as they get older?

What I Noticed

I was happy that David and Chuck realized that they needed to keep the Basidiumites a secret in order to protect the mushroom planet they had come to love.

What did you notice?

 Quotes

"Insanity: doing the same thing over and over again and expecting different results."
—ALBERT EINSTEIN

 Next

Check out these other titles:

The Lives of Christopher Chant
BY DIANA WYNNE JONES

The Monster Garden
BY VIVIEN ALCOCK

The Moorchild
BY ELOISE MCGRAW

So You Want to Be a Wizard
BY DIANE DUANE

Space Race
BY SYLVIA WAUGH

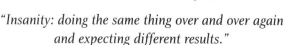

PART II
Subject Conversations

> " Keep it simple, but never simplify. "
>
> —ALBERT EINSTEIN

The premise of *Reading Together* embraces the notion of talking together. Many of the language skills children need to become good readers are first learned in conversation. Vocabulary acquired through conversation is essential to literacy, and conversations are where children learn to think and express themselves, honing their creative and critical thinking skills. The Subject Conversation questions go from the simple, not simplistic, to the more complex, all in the effort of keeping a conversation going. They avoid questions that can be answered with a yes or no—yes or no questions take you into a cul-de-sac, and the conversation ends before it really begins.

The Subject Conversation questions encourage reflection and give children the language they need to express themselves and broaden the conversations found on the Story Pages. For example, when a child reads a book where popularity is the main subject of the story, moving to the Subject Conversation questions on "popularity" expands their thoughts about popularity. The Subject Conversation questions show a child she has something to say about a subject, and that the subject doesn't just exist in a book. The Subject Conversations, combined with the conversations on the Story Pages, encourage children to see connections between their thoughts and the books they read. Children who are able to see the relationship between a subject in their lives and a subject in a book are children who better understand what they read. This is how children become more competent and confident readers.

The best books are always about more than one subject, therefore I chose not to link titles with specific subjects. If you want to find a book on a specific subject, the World of Ideas section on the Story Pages lists the subjects that book explores.

Tips for Using the Subject Conversations

★ The questions are framed to take you further into the conversation. None of these questions are meant to offer quick answers.

★ The questions are not meant to be vehicles for how to improve your child.

★ The Subject Conversations encourage children, who are concrete thinkers and who do not easily grasp complexities and shades of gray, to see that there are not always easy answers, that every stick has two ends.

★ It is okay to ask a question that has an obvious answer—it provides an ease of entry into a conversation.

★ Often a conversation you have on a subject can lead to a book recommendation, maybe even to a child's home-run book!

★ A good conversation can be all of two minutes. The questions serve as prompts that allow the conversation to go as long as someone has something meaningful to say.

Subject Conversations

Adversity	Envy	Luck
Appreciation	Fairness	Lying
Attitude	Fear	Making a Difference
Blame	Feelings	Manners
Bullies	Forgiveness	Mistakes
Challenges	Friendship	Passion
Choice	Generosity	Peer Pressure
Confidence	Gossip	Perseverance
Courage	Happiness	Popularity
Death	Heroes and Heroines	Praise
Disappointment	Hope	Prejudice
Discipline	Humor	Promises
Doing Your Best	Integrity	Responsibility
Empathy	Kindness	Self-Reliance

ADVERSITY

*"People are like teabags; you never know how strong they are
until you put them in hot water."*
—RITA MAE BROWN

★ Are *misfortune, crisis, catastrophe, tough luck, bad break, bummer,* and *hardship*
other words for adversity?

★ Do you believe there is always something you can learn from any situation
and use it to your advantage? Can you think of a hardship you learned
from?

★ How could a difficult situation be an opportunity to do your best?

★ Is a crisis a terrible thing to waste?

APPRECIATION

"Most human beings have an almost infinite capacity for taking things for granted."
—ALDOUS HUXLEY

★ Can you appreciate something you take for granted?
  ☆ What do you take for granted?

★ Can you appreciate something you feel entitled to?

★ Does entitlement get in the way of appreciation?
  ☆ What are you entitled to?

★ Is appreciation an attitude, a choice, or a habit?
  ☆ What do you appreciate? Why do you appreciate it?
  ☆ What does "count your blessings" mean?

ATTITUDE

"Life is what we make it—always has been, always will be."
—GRANDMA MOSES

★ Do you choose your attitudes? How hard is it to choose an attitude that works for you and not against you?
  ☆ Is choosing the right attitude a habit you can acquire?

★ Can you think of a situation where something went wrong but you kept the right attitude?

★ What does it mean when someone says, "you need a new attitude"?
  ☆ Is it easy to change your attitude?
  ☆ How can changing your attitude change a situation? Is it more about getting dealt the right cards or playing well the cards you are dealt?

★ Where do you get your attitudes from—your friends, the media, your family, your religion?

BLAME

"To err is human, to blame the next guy even more so."
—UNKNOWN

★ What other words could you substitute for blame—*technically it's not my fault, I didn't mean to, she made me do it?*

★ What purpose does blame serve? Does blame ever help a situation?
　☆ Why is it so easy to blame someone else? How do you feel when you have someone to point the finger at?
　☆ Does it make a difference whose fault it is?

★ Is the opposite of blame a willingness to take responsibility?
　☆ When is it time to stop blaming and deal with the facts?

BULLIES

"[T]he essential thing with a bully is they're unhappy."
—MARY STOLZ

★ Are you born a bully?

★ Do boys and girls bully in the same way?

★ Why does a person become a bully?

★ Did you ever meet a happy bully?

★ Do bullies have "genuine" friends?

★ Do you know a bully? Can you stand up to this bully? Can you ignore this bully? Can you change this bully? Do you understand why they bully?
　☆ Could you make this bully a friend?

CHALLENGES

"It is not the mountain we conquer but ourselves."
—SIR EDMUND HILLARY

★ What qualities do you need to meet challenges successfully—*tenacity, the right attitude, confidence, boldness, vigor, discipline, guts, patience, moxie, resilience?*
   ☆ Which of these qualities comes naturally to you? Which ones don't?

★ Is it ever a good idea not to take on a challenge?

★ Do you take on too many challenges or not enough challenges?

★ What challenges are you most proud of?

CHOICE

*"You have brains in your head. You have feet in your shoes.
You can steer yourself any direction you choose."*
—DR. SEUSS

★ Do you use your head or your heart to make a choice?

★ Are you responsible for your choices?

★ Is not making a choice making a choice?
   ☆ Does every choice have a consequence?

★ Does making the right choice always make you feel good?
   ☆ Can you think of a situation when you made the right choice and it made you feel good?
   ☆ Can you think of a situation when you made the right choice and it didn't make you feel good?

★ Why are some choices harder than others? How does ambivalence complicate a choice?

CONFIDENCE

"Experience tells you what to do; confidence allows you to do it."
—STAN SMITH

★ Are you born with confidence?
  ☆ Where does confidence come from, yourself or others?
  ☆ Can somebody give you confidence?

★ Is confidence an attitude? If you think you are confident, does that make it so?

★ Are people who appear confident actually confident?
  ☆ Are people who brag confident?

★ Can you have too much confidence? What happens when you are overconfident?

★ What do you feel confident about? What don't you feel confident about?

COURAGE

"One man with courage makes a majority."
—ANDREW JACKSON

★ Does courage always have to be daring, gallant, and bold? Can courage be quiet, soft, and subtle?
  ☆ Can saying no be courageous?

★ Can anyone be courageous?

★ Can being courageous get you in trouble? Are there times when acting courageously is not a good idea?

★ In what situations do you find it hard to act courageous?
  ☆ Are there situations in which you find it easy to act courageous?

DEATH

"That it will never come again is what makes life so sweet."
—EMILY DICKINSON

★ People express sadness in many different ways. What do you do when you are sad?
　☆ When you are sad, how do you make yourself feel better?

★ Is sad a feeling you try to ignore? What happens when you try to ignore a feeling?
　☆ Do you cry easily? How do you feel after you have a good cry?

★ In your family do you have traditions and rituals that keep a person's memory alive—lighting a candle, planting a tree, saying a special prayer, telling stories about a person, following their ideals?

★ Do you believe that someone you loved will always be with you in spirit?

★ Would you want to live forever? What would be the benefits? What would be the disadvantages?

DISAPPOINTMENT

"Zeus does not bring all men's plans to fulfillment."
—HOMER

★ What are other words for disappointment—*frustration, disillusionment, discontent, letdown*?

★ How do you react to disappointment? Do you ignore it, use it to spur you on, feel defeated by it, let it curb your expectations, or get angry because of it?

★ What is a big disappointment? What is a little disappointment?

★ Do you avoid trying something so you will not be disappointed?

★ What is more difficult, disappointment in yourself or another?

★ Can it be possible to never be disappointed?

DISCIPLINE

"The ability to concentrate and to use your time well is everything."
—LEE IACOCCA

★ What other words could you substitute for discipline—*diligence, fortitude, willpower, focus, concentration?*

★ Are you disciplined at some things but not at others? Why?
  ☆ Do you have to like doing something in order to be disciplined?
  ☆ Can you achieve anything without discipline?
  ☆ Can you ever be too disciplined?

★ Why is it easy to become distracted?
  ☆ What gets you back on track? What strategies do you use to get your focus back?
  ☆ Can distractions serve a useful purpose?
  ☆ What are your biggest distractions?

★ When is it hard for you to be disciplined? When is it easy for you to be disciplined?

DOING YOUR BEST

"If we all did the things we are capable of doing, we would literally astound ourselves."
—THOMAS ALVA EDISON

★ Is it important to give your best effort to all things—even those things you do not like to do?
  ☆ How do you feel when you do not do your best?

★ Does doing your best guarantee success? How do you feel when you do your best and you fail?
  ☆ How do you feel when you have not done your best and you fail?

★ Do you do your best for you or for someone else?

EMPATHY

"Do not judge your fellow man until you have stood in his place."
—HILLEL

★ What other words could you substitute for empathy—*compassion, understanding, pity, kindness, consideration, sympathy, unselfishness*?

★ Is thinking about a person's well-being the same thing as doing something about it? Does empathy require action?

★ Do you have to like a person to have empathy for them?

★ Can you think of a situation when you put yourself in someone else's shoes? How did it change your perspective?

★ What would the world look like if nobody was able to have empathy for others?

ENVY

"Envy is the art of counting the other fellow's blessings instead of your own."
—HAROLD COFFIN

★ What are other words for envy—*wanting, discontent, greed, desire, wishfulness, jealousy, the green-eyed monster*?

★ Can you want what somebody has and not be envious of them?
　☆ Do you want something because you want it, or do you want something because your friend has it?

★ Is there a good side of envy?
　☆ Can envy motivate you?

★ Can envy make you happy? Does envy serve you well?

★ Can envy make you unhappy? Does envy bring discontent?

★ Can you envy someone and not be jealous?

FAIRNESS

"If each person sweeps in front of his or her own door, the whole street is clean."
—YIDDISH PROVERB

★ Do you think life is fair? Do you expect life to be fair? Is life meant to be fair?
  ☆ Do you believe "what goes around, comes around"? Does that make life fair?

★ When you feel life isn't fair, do you get mad? Do you let it go? Do you try to make it fair?

★ Does "fair" enter into every aspect of life—school, work, friendships, sports?

★ What is one of the most unfair situations you have encountered? Did your friends and family think it was unfair, too?
  ☆ Can you think of a situation that was completely fair?

FEAR

"No passion so effectively robs the mind of all its powers of acting and reasoning as fear."
—EDMUND BURKE

★ What are you afraid of—the first day of school, sleepaway camp, staying overnight at a friend's house, trying different foods, doing an activity without a friend?

★ Do your fears prevent you from trying new things?
  ☆ What do you discover when you do the very thing you were afraid of— you survived, you gained confidence, it wasn't so scary?

★ If you walked away from everything you feared, how many new things would you never try? What makes it hard to try new things?
  ☆ Is there a certain amount of worry, fear, and hesitation in doing anything new?

★ Does fear ever serve a good purpose? Can fear keep you safe?

READING TOGETHER

FEELINGS

"A mother understands what a child does not say."
—JEWISH PROVERB

★ How many feelings can you name—*pride, shame, joy, guilt, excitement, fear, embarrassment, satisfaction, melancholy, shy, content, lonely, envy, disappointment?*
   ☆ You can't see or smell your feelings. Where are they?

★ What happens when you ignore your feelings? Can you ignore your feelings?

★ Do you need to share your feelings with others all the time? Are some feelings more private than others?

★ Are feelings ever silly? Can you argue with a person's feelings?

★ Do you always know what you are feeling and why you feel that way?
   ☆ What would it be like if everyone in your class had to wear a badge showing what kind of mood they were in? Would you like it?

FORGIVENESS

"Nobody ever forgets where he buried a hatchet."
—KIN HUBBARD

★ Are *revenge, blame, retaliation, holding a grudge, vengeance,* and *reprisal* the opposite of forgiveness?

★ Which is more difficult: saying "I'm sorry" to a friend or accepting a friend's "I'm sorry"?
   ☆ Are there consequences for not accepting an apology? Are there consequences for not offering an apology?
   ☆ Who gets hurt most in not forgiving?

★ Can you forgive someone who has not asked for your forgiveness?

★ Does anyone owe you an apology? Do you owe anyone an apology?

FRIENDSHIP

"A friend is a person with whom I may be sincere. Before him I may think aloud."
—RALPH WALDO EMERSON

★ What are some qualities you look for in a friend—loyalty, trust, compatibility, respect, sincerity?

★ Describe your best friend. What makes that person your best friend?
  ☆ Are your friends similar to you or different from you?
  ☆ Do all of your friends have to like each other?
  ☆ Do you like to have lots of friends or a few close friends?
  ☆ Do you feel responsible for the actions of your friends?

★ Do you have to be friends with everyone?

★ Do friendships change? Can you outgrow a friendship?
  ☆ What makes getting out of a friendship difficult?
  ☆ How much are you willing to compromise to keep a friendship?

★ Would you tell your friend something that might jeopardize the friendship?

GENEROSITY

"Generosity lies less in giving much than in giving at the right moment."
—JEAN DE LA BRUYÉRE

★ Is generosity only giving tangible things? Can you be generous with your emotions?
  ☆ Can giving someone a smile, a hug, or a kind word at the right moment be considered generous?

★ When you give something you don't need or want, is that being generous?

★ Does generosity need to be repaid with generosity?

★ When have you found it easy to be generous?
  ☆ When have you found it difficult to be generous?

★ Is generosity a privilege or an obligation?

READING TOGETHER

GOSSIP

"What you don't see with your eyes, don't invent with your mouth."
—JEWISH PROVERB

★ What are other words for gossip—*slander, chitchat, defamation, hearsay, idle talk, rumor?*

★ What is the difference between gossip and telling what happened?
   ☆ Is gossip always malicious?
   ☆ Can gossip help a person's reputation? Can it ruin a person's reputation?
   ☆ If what you are saying about a person is true, does that make it "right" to say it?

★ How does gossiping about a person make you feel?
   ☆ If you are not the one gossiping but the one listening, are you promoting gossip?

★ Do your friends gossip? Do you find it hard to stay clear of gossip?

★ Why do people gossip?

HAPPINESS

"I prayed for wonders instead of happiness and you gave them to me."
—ABRAHAM HESCHEL

★ Is it possible to be happy all the time? Would you want to be happy all the time?

★ Does happiness come from the "outside" or is it an "inside" job?
   ☆ Does happiness depend on circumstance or disposition?
   ☆ How do friends, culture, advertisements, and media influence your definition of happiness?

★ Do porch swings, fluffy pillows, making a sand castle, eating mangos, owls hooting, climbing a tree, or riding on a train make you happy?

★ What in life do you need to be happy?
   ☆ Name eleven things that make you happy.

HEROES AND HEROINES

"To have no heroes is to have no aspirations."
—CHARLES HORTON COOLEY

★ Heroes and heroines remind us of who we are and who we might become.
　☆ What are some of their qualities?
　☆ Are heroes and heroines bold, brave, noble, and courageous? Are they also independent, intelligent, compassionate, tenacious, witty, and competent?

★ What is the difference between a hero or heroine and a celebrity? Do celebrities need to be celebrated? Do they need attention, recognition, and fame?

★ How can a hero or heroine change the world in small, unnoticed ways? Is this the definition of an unsung hero?
　☆ Can you name someone who is an unsung hero?

★ Who would be on your list of heroes and heroines?

HOPE

"Hope is one of those things in life you cannot do without."
—LEROY DOUGLAS

★ What are other words for hope—*optimism, confidence, dreams, wishes, expectation, trust, faith, idealism?*

★ Are you born with a hopeful attitude or do you develop a hopeful attitude?

★ How can hope change a situation? Can hope make a bad day a little bit better?

★ What would your life look like without hope? Can you live without hope?

★ What are your hopes?

HUMOR

"Imagination was given to man to compensate him for what he is not; a sense of humor to console him for what he is."
—SIR FRANCIS BACON

★ Are you born with a sense of humor?

★ Is it possible to have friends without a sense of humor?

★ How does a sense of humor change a situation?
   ☆ What makes it hard to find humor when you are upset or annoyed? Is that the most important time to have a sense of humor?

★ Who do you know who has the best sense of humor?

★ Do you have a sense of humor about yourself?
   ☆ Have you ever lost your sense of humor? How did you get it back?

INTEGRITY

"If you don't stand for something, you'll fall for anything."
—MICHAEL EVANS

★ What other words could you substitute for integrity—*truth, honor, ethics, principle, trust, sense of right and wrong*?

★ What is more important, what people say or what people do?
   ☆ What happens when your actions do not coincide with your principles?
   ☆ Has there ever been a situation when your principle of right and wrong was tested?

★ Having integrity, following your beliefs, and acting on your principles should be the easiest things in the world. Why do you think it is difficult to act with integrity?
   ☆ What makes acting with integrity difficult—you don't want to offend a friend, you don't want to "rock the boat," or you don't want to put yourself on the line?

KINDNESS

"Then I thought about how the kind act can be big and dramatic or so small that only one person notices, like a smile at a hard moment. A bowl of berries."
—LYNNE RAE PERKINS

★ What other words could you substitute for kindness—*generosity, charity, thoughtfulness, consideration, goodness, sympathy, understanding, compassion, big-heartedness*?

★ How do you learn to be a kind person?
☆ Are there situations when it is easy to be kind?
☆ Are there situations when it is difficult to be kind?

★ What makes kindness important? How does kindness change a situation?
☆ How would not being kind change a situation?

★ Do you repay kindness with kindness?

★ Who is the kindest person you know?

LUCK

"I think when I work 14 hours a day, seven days a week, I get lucky."
—ARMAND HAMMER

★ What are other words for luck—*good fortune, fate, destiny, coincidence, fluke*?

★ Are you born lucky or do you make your own luck?
☆ Do you think you are lucky?
☆ If you think you are lucky, are you lucky?
☆ Do lucky charms work? Do you have a lucky charm?

★ Can you depend on luck?

★ Can you give someone else luck?

★ Is it possible to push one's luck?

LYING

"Oh what a tangled web we weave, when first we practice to deceive."
—SIR WALTER SCOTT

★ Why do people lie?
　☆ Can lies make a situation better? Can lies make a situation worse?

★ Do the motives of why a person lies make a difference?
　☆ If you tell a friend a lie to make them feel better, does that make it okay to lie? Are these white lies?

★ Is it hard to get out of a lie? Does one lie often lead to another lie?
　☆ Do you need a really good memory to lie?

★ How do you feel when you find out someone has lied to you?
　☆ What makes it hard to trust someone after they lie?

MAKING A DIFFERENCE

"All we can do during our lives is to leave a trace. We can leave it on a piece of paper, or on the ground, or in the hearts and minds of others."
—ELIE WIESEL

★ What does making a difference mean to you?

★ Is wanting to make a difference something you are born with or something you develop?

★ What would the world be like if no one thought about making a difference?
　☆ Is indifference or not caring the opposite of making a difference?

★ Do you have to do something "big" to make a difference?
　☆ Can a smile make a difference to someone?

★ Do you always know when you make a difference?

★ What are some of the ways you can make a difference in someone's day?

★ How could someone make a difference in your day?

MANNERS

"Children act in the village as they have learned at home."
—SWEDISH PROVERB

★ Good manners are the way people show respect. Where do you get your manners?
  ☆ Are manners, whether good or bad, a habit?
  ☆ Should manners be saved for special occasions?
  ☆ Do people judge you on your manners?
  ☆ Can good manners help in a difficult situation?

★ Can you think of a situation when good manners made a difference?
  ☆ Can you think of a situation when good manners would have made a difference?

MISTAKES

"Experience is the name everyone gives to their mistakes."
—OSCAR WILDE

★ Can you go through life and never make mistakes?
  ☆ Do you think it is possible to be perfect?
  ☆ Is perfection boring? Is there risk, fun, and adventure in perfection?

★ What makes it difficult to practice Winston Churchill's maxim: "Success is the ability to go from one failure to another with no loss of enthusiasm"?

★ How do you feel when you make a mistake—embarrassed, foolish, stupid?
  ☆ Do you try to deny or defend your mistakes?
  ☆ What makes it hard to be enthusiastic about mistakes?

★ Does the fear of making mistakes make you less willing to try new things or take risks?

PASSION

"Nothing great in the world has been accomplished without passion."
—GEORG WILHELM FRIEDRICH HEGEL

★ What are other words for passion—*zeal, excitement, devotion, fervor, infatuation, obsession?*

★ Are passions created or discovered or both? How do you find your passion?
　☆ Is passion more about why you do something than what you do?
　☆ Can you be passionate about something you do not like?
　☆ Can you be passionate about everything? Do your passions change?

★ Can someone help you find a passion? Can you help someone find a passion?

★ What are your passions?
　☆ What are you parents' passions? What are your friends' passions?

PEER PRESSURE

"Nobody ever grows up in a group."
—RICHARD PECK

★ How willing are you to be different? Does being different make you uncomfortable?

★ What makes it hard to go against the majority?

★ Have there been times when you've felt you had to go against the crowd to do things your own way?
　☆ Is it easier to conform?
　☆ Are there consequences for going along with the crowd?
　☆ Are there consequences for not going along with the crowd?

★ What happens when fitting in becomes more important than being yourself?
　☆ Why are we influenced by what others do and think?

★ Does a person ever outgrow peer pressure?
　☆ Are adults immune from peer pressure?

PERSEVERANCE

"Either do not attempt at all, or go through with it."
—OVID

★ Do you need *resilience, determination, stamina, drive, stubbornness, willpower,* and *endurance* to persevere? What other qualities do you need?

★ Do you only persevere at things you think you are good at?

★ Do you only persevere with things that you like?

★ Do you find it difficult to persevere with things you don't like?

★ How does encouragement and praise help you to persevere?
  ☆ How much encouragement and praise do you need—a little or a lot?

★ Does perseverance always guarantee success?

POPULARITY

"The only thing worse than being talked about is not being talked about."
—OSCAR WILDE

★ What does it mean to be popular?
  ☆ Is being *well-liked, accepted,* and *admired* the same as being popular?
  ☆ Does being popular mean you have many friends?

★ How important is it to be popular?

★ Who decides who is popular?
  ☆ If you are popular, will you be popular forever?

★ Who decides who is unpopular?
  ☆ If you are unpopular, will you be unpopular forever?

PRAISE

*"Honest criticism is hard to take, particularly from a relative,
a friend, an acquaintance, or a stranger."*
—FRANKLIN P. JONES

★ What is the difference between praise and encouragement? Is praise a compliment and encouragement support?
☆ When do you need praise and when do you need encouragement?

★ Does praise feel best when it comes from somebody who knows the effort you put into an accomplishment?
☆ Can praise be insincere? Would you call that flattery?

★ How useful is criticism? Can it be more useful than praise?

★ Is there such a thing as too much praise?
☆ Is there such a thing as too little praise?

★ Can you think of a situation when the praise you received made a difference?
☆ Can you think of a situation when a little bit of praise would have made a difference?

PREJUDICE

*"We hate some persons because we do not know them,
and will not know them because we hate them."*
—CHARLES CALEB COLTON

★ What are other words for prejudice—*snap judgments, narrow-mindedness, bias, preconceived ideas, intolerance, discrimination*?

★ How do you define prejudice? What do you get when you take apart the word *prejudice*—pre-judge?
☆ How does stereotyping promote prejudice?
☆ How does bias promote prejudice?
☆ How do ignorance and fear promote prejudice?

★ Is prejudice always about people's differences, such as gender, religion, class, nationality, or race? Why are people afraid of what's different?

★ Why is it hard to overcome prejudice? How does a person become less prejudiced?
☆ Do tolerance and acceptance make it difficult to be prejudiced?

★ How do empathy and compassion for a person make it more difficult to have prejudice about them?
☆ Can you have empathy and compassion for someone you don't know?

★ You can pass laws that make prejudice illegal, but does that change people's feelings?

PROMISES

"He who is slowest in making a promise is most faithful in its performance."
—JEAN JACQUES ROUSSEAU

★ Do you have to keep a promise?
☆ Are promises that are made lightly easily broken?
☆ Is it sometimes easier to make a promise than to say, "No, I can't"?

★ How do you get out of a promise?
☆ Does "I forgot" or "I am too busy" make it okay to break a promise?

★ How do you feel when you break a promise?
☆ How do you feel when someone breaks a promise to you?

RESPONSIBILITY

"No snowflake in an avalanche ever feels responsible."
—VOLTAIRE

★ Is being accountable for your actions a good definition of responsibility?
☆ Is accepting a responsibility a contract?
☆ What makes it difficult to get out of a responsibility?

★ Is being dependable part of being responsible? What about being conscientious and reliable?

★ Do you get confidence from being responsible?
  ☆ Do you get praise from being responsible?
  ☆ Do you get more privileges from being responsible?

★ What are you responsible for in your home?
  ☆ Did you choose this responsibility or were you assigned this responsibility?
  ☆ Do you like to be responsible?

SELF-RELIANCE

"The best bet is to bet on yourself."
—ARNOLD GLASOW

★ What are other words for self-reliant—*independent, resourceful, capable, confident?*

★ Where do you learn to be self-reliant and resourceful—by having everything done for you or by doing things for yourself?
  ☆ Why does it feel good to do things for yourself?

★ At what age do you become self-reliant?
  ☆ Can you be self-reliant in some things but not in other things?

★ In what situations are you self-reliant?
  ☆ In what situations do you want to become self-reliant?

102 and Beyond

One would think that choosing 101 books would satisfy my passion for getting the right books into the right hands, but alas, it has not. I found too many wonderful books not mentioned and I just couldn't let that happen. This is not intended to be a complete list of books—just some of my personal favorites and some favorites from children. The twenty-six categories are listed by genre to help you and your child easily find a book on a subject of interest. Other than titles listed in the category If the Shoe Fits, I purposely did not assign specific grade levels because I wanted a child's curiosity to be the motivation for choosing a book. Many of these books easily fit into several categories. A title that appears in Curiosity Didn't Kill the Cat could also easily fit into Is This a True Story? or You Can't Eat Just One. I am often surprised at the idiosyncratic way people categorize books, and I am just as eccentric as everyone else. How I grouped the books is crystal clear to me but might cause you to raise your eyebrows. That's part of the fun. Categorize the books however you like—the important thing is that you enjoy them as much as I have. These books work with children—meaning children like them and have plenty to say about them. Enjoy these books and add your own favorites to the list.

A BANQUET OF ILLUSTRATIONS AND STORIES

"Oh, I loved that book as a child!" Picture storybooks are a child's first love and the books they will remember. They are the books they will return to as adults with their own children. Don't even think of making the mistake that as soon as children learn to read we need to wean them from one of mankind's greatest achievements—the picture book! Nothing lasts longer in memory than a child's first love of a story. These books become their literary inheritance.

And to Think That I Saw It on Mulberry Street, by Dr. Seuss

Animal Faces, by Akira Satoh and Kyoko Toda

Doctor De Soto, by William Steig

Harry the Dirty Dog, by Gene Zion

The House on East 88th Street, by Bernard Waber

Leo the Late Bloomer, by Ruth Krauss

Lilly's Purple Plastic Purse, by Kevin Henkes

Millions of Cats, by Wanda Gag

The Moon in My Room, by Uri Shulevitz

Mr. Gumpy's Outing, by John Burningham

Owl Moon, by Jane Yolen

Seven Blind Mice, by Ed Young

Sylvester and the Magic Pebble, by William Steig

The Treasure, by Uri Shulevitz

"I THINK I CAN, I THINK I CAN"

The nursery is where readers are made. It is never too early to start reading to children and surrounding them with books. In developing the skill of reading there is nothing better than a good story. The more you read, the better reader you become—practice makes permanent.

Amelia Bedelia, by Peggy Parish

Chester, by Syd Hoff

Daniel's Duck, by Clyde Robert Bulla

Eat My Dust! Henry Ford's First Race, by Monica Kulling

The Fire Cat, by Esther Averill

George and Martha, by James Marshall

Henry and Mudge, by Cynthia Rylant

Hill of Fire, by Thomas P. Lewis

Little Bear, by Else Holmelund Minarik

Minnie and Moo: The Case of the Missing Jelly Donut, by Denys Cazet

Nate the Great, by Marjorie Weinman Sharmat

Mr. Putter and Tabby, by Cynthia Rylant

Sam the Minuteman, by Nathaniel Benchley

LET'S START AT THE VERY BEGINNING

Memorizing letter shapes and giving them names with flash cards can be boring, so why not make it fun? If you thought counting from 1 to 100 was routine and you only knew the musical "ABCDEFG, now I know my ABCs," then you haven't seen some of these marvelous books for having fun with the 123s and ABCs.

Alphabet City, by Stephen T. Johnson

Anno's Mysterious Multiplying Jar, by Mitsumasa Anno

The Disappearing Alphabet, by Richard Wilbur

Firefighters A to Z, by Chris L. Demarest

Gone Wild, by David McLimans

The Graphic Alphabet, by David Pelletier

The Handmade Alphabet, by Laura Rankin

How Much Is a Million?, by David Schwartz

On Beyond Zebra, by Dr. Seuss

On Market Street, by Arnold Lobel

One Is a Snail, Ten Is a Crab, by April Pulley Sayre

When Sheep Cannot Sleep: The Counting Book, by Satoshi Kitamura

PICTURES SPEAK WHEN THERE ARE NO WORDS

How do you read a wordless or nearly wordless picture book? Without words, the shapes, lines, and colors tell the story. One of the great things about wordless picture books is that children at any age can read them by telling the story *they* see in each picture. Share with your child the story *you* see in the pictures. Where did the story take you and where did the story take your child? Without words, the story unfolds for each reader in its own unique way. Don't miss the opportunity of knowing these delightful reads simply because you didn't know what to do with them.

Anno's USA, by Mitsumasa Anno

Flotsam, by David Wiesner

Good Dog, Carl, by Alexandra Day

In the Town All Year Round, by Rotraut Susanne Berner

Mrs. Mustard's Baby Faces, by Jane Wattenberg

Museum Trip, by Barbara Lehman

Polo: The Runaway Book, by Regis Faller

Rainstorm, by Barbara Lehman

Sector 7, by David Wiesner

The Silver Pony, by Lynd Ward

The Snowman, by Raymond Briggs

Wave, by Suzy Lee

Zoom, by Istvan Banyai

IF THE SHOE FITS

Grade 2+

To avoid the sand trap of a good book at the wrong time, follow the five-finger rule. If a child meets five or more words on a page they don't know and can't figure out, they are probably a bit too young for this book. Don't push—come back to the book at a future time. The right book at the right time keeps the pages turning.

26 Fairmont Avenue, by Tomie de Paola

Absolutely Lucy, by Ilene Cooper

Atlantis: The Lost City, by Andrew Donkin

The Bravest Dog Ever: The True Story of Balto, by Natalie Standiford

The Case of the Dirty Clue, by George E. Stanley

The Chalk Box Kid, by Clyde Robert Bulla

Ivy and Bean, by Annie Barrows

Kate Shelley and the Midnight Express, by Margaret K. Wetterer

Morgy Makes His Move, by Maggie Lewis

Moxy Maxwell Does Not Love Stuart Little, by Peggy Gifford

Ned Mouse Breaks Away, by Tim Wynne-Jones

Prairie School, by Avi

Tornado, by Betsy Byars

Grade 4+

People often think that by the time a child reaches fourth grade their reading skills would allow them to read everything. Not so—they are still honing their skills. This is the age when we begin to see attrition in reading because there is a tendency to assume children should be reading harder books. Children at this age need books that deliver a great story, capture an older child's interest, and are accessible to read.

Because of Winn-Dixie, by Kate DiCamillo

The Big Wave, by Pearl S. Buck

Bull Run, by Paul Fleischman

Charlotte's Web, by E. B. White

The Cricket in Times Square, by George Selden

Diary of a Wimpy Kid, by Jeff Kinney

The Enormous Egg, by Oliver Butterworth

The Friendship, by Mildred D. Taylor

The Giant Rat of Sumatra, by Sid Fleischman

The Houdini Box, by Brian Selznick

The Incredible Journey, by Sheila Burnford

The Pushcart War, by Jean Merrill

The Tale of Despereaux, by Kate DiCamillo

IS THIS A TRUE STORY?

I have found that one of the best ways to capture a child's curiosity is to read them a true story. When they ask, "Is that true? Did it really happen?" and you're able to say yes, they get hooked. These stories are based on true events and as we all know the best of fiction, those made-up stories, often come from real life. Did you know the book *The Little Red Lighthouse* is about a real lighthouse that still stands today under the George Washington Bridge in New York City?

All Stations Distress! April 15, 1912: The Day the Titanic Sank, by Don Brown

Blizzard!, by Jim Murphy

Duel!: Burr and Hamilton's Deadly War of Words, by Dennis Brindell Fradin

Fly High!: The Story of Bessie Coleman, by Louise Borden and Mary Kay Kroeger

How It Was with Dooms: A True Story from Africa, by Xan Hopcraft

The Journey That Saved Curious George, by Louise Borden

Koko's Kitten, by Dr. Francine Patterson

Lady Liberty: A Biography, by Doreen Rappaport

The Little Red Lighthouse and the Great Gray Bridge, by Hildegarde H. Swift

Passage to Freedom: The Sugihara Story, by Ken Mochizuki

Shipwreck at the Bottom of the World, by Jennifer Armstrong

Who Was First?: Discovering the Americas, by Russell Freedman

MORE GOES ON IN THE DUGOUT THAN ON THE FIELD

A popular request from both boys and girls are books on sports. The best sports books offer more than the story of a game and the skills needed to play the game well—they offer a blueprint of what it means to be part of a team and how to be a good sport.

America's Champion Swimmer: Gertrude Ederle, by David A. Adler

Babe and Me: A Baseball Card Adventure, by Dan Gutman

Dirt on Their Skirts, by Doreen Rappaport

The Greatest: Muhammad Ali, by Walter Dean Myers

Heat, by Mike Lupica

Home Run: The Story of Babe Ruth, by Robert Burleigh

In the Year of the Boar and Jackie Robinson, by Bette Bao Lord

Keeping Score, by Linda Sue Park

Lives of the Athletes, by Kathleen Krull

Lou Gehrig: The Luckiest Man, by David A. Adler

The Suitcase, by Mildred Pitts Walter

We Are the Ship: The Story of Negro League Baseball, by Kadir Nelson

Wilma Unlimited: How Wilma Rudolph Became the World's Fastest Woman, by
Kathleen Krull

ONE LIFE IS NOT ENOUGH!

Who doesn't like to eavesdrop on the lives of others? Who doesn't like to travel
to new places? Who doesn't like to learn about the past? Illustrated biographies
tap into a child's inquisitiveness and showcase information that could easily be
in an encyclopedia (but how enjoyable is it to read an encyclopedia?). What
better way to read a story about Thomas Edison than a book filled not only with
information but also with pictures of people and places and copies of letters
written long ago! Here are some of my favorite biographies.

The Adventures of Marco Polo, by Russell Freedman

The Big Book of Dummies, Rebels and Other Geniuses, by Jean-Bernard Pouy
and Serge Bloch

Confucius: The Golden Rule, by Russell Freedman

Helen's Eyes: A Photobiography of Annie Sullivan, Helen Keller's Teacher, by
Marfe Ferguson Delano

Inventing the Future: A Photobiography of Thomas Alva Edison,
by Marfe Ferguson Delano

Leonardo: Beautiful Dreamer, by Robert Byrd

The Lincolns: A Scrapbook Look at Abraham and Mary, by Candace Fleming

Rachel: The Story of Rachel Carson, by Amy Ehrlich

Saladin: Noble Prince of Islam, by Diane Stanley

Starry Messenger: Galileo Galilei, by Peter Sís

Tree of Life: Charles Darwin, by Peter Sís

Traveling Man: The Journey of Ibn Battuta 1325–1354, by James Rumford

What's the Big Idea, Ben Franklin?, by Jean Fritz

CURIOSITY DIDN'T KILL THE CAT

The cat may not die from curiosity, but without it, the cat would surely perish. Reading should inspire curiosity—it shouldn't become a chore and a bore and something necessary just to complete an assignment. Here are some of my favorite nonfiction books that keep the sheer pleasure of learning alive. These books capture the moment in childhood when the wider awareness of the world and wonder coexist.

The American Story: 100 True Tales from American History,
     by Jennifer Armstrong

Girls Think of Everything: Stories of Ingenious Inventions by Women,
     by Catherine Thimmesh

A Little History of the World, by E. H. Gombrich

Mistakes That Worked, by Charlotte Jones

The New Way Things Work, by David Macaulay

Our White House: Looking In, Looking Out, by the NCBLA

Out of Sight: Pictures of Hidden Worlds, by Seymour Simon

The Scrambled States of America, by Laurie Keller

Signers: The 56 Stories Behind the Declaration of Independence,
     by Dennis Brindell Fradin

Team Moon: How 400,000 People Landed Apollo 11 on the Moon,
     by Catherine Thimmesh

The Top of the World: Climbing Mount Everest, by Steve Jenkins

What the World Eats, by Faith D'Aluisio

NATURE'S RIDDLES

It's been said that, according to the laws of aerodynamics, bumblebees should not be able to fly. They do not have the capacity in terms of wing size or beats per second to achieve flight. The origin of this myth has been difficult to pin down with any certainty—it's a conundrum. For children enthralled with nature and science, these books offer awesome information.

The Case of the Mummified Pigs: And Other Mysteries in Nature,
    by Susan E. Quinlan

Girls Who Looked Under Rocks: The Lives of Six Pioneering Naturalists,
    by Jeannine Atkins

Gorilla Doctors: Saving Endangered Great Apes, by Pamela S. Turner

Great Scientists, by Jacqueline Fortey

The Magic School Bus Inside the Earth, by Joanna Cole

The Reason for a Flower, by Ruth Heller

Secrets of Sound: Studying the Calls and Songs of Whales, Elephants, and Birds,
    by April Pulley Sayre

The Sense of Wonder, by Rachel Carson

The Tarantula Scientist, by Sy Montgomery

What Do You Do With a Tail Like This?, by Robin Page

What Does the Crow Know? Mysteries of Animal Intelligence,
    by Margery Facklam

Ice Bears, by Brenda Z. Guiberson

YOU CAN'T EAT JUST ONE

Children are born collectors—be it baseball cards, dolls, rocks, comic books, marbles, or even books! Children need and want familiarity and independence in their reading, hence the popularity and almost manic love for books in a series. Here are some of my favories:

The Allie Finkle's Rules for Girls series, by Meg Cabot

The Anastasia series, by Lois Lowry

The Baseball Card Adventure series, by Dan Gutman

The Children of Green Knowe series, by L. M. Boston

The Encyclopedia Brown series, by Donald J. Sobol

The Hermux Tantamoq Adventures series, by Michael Hoeye

The Littles series, by John Peterson

The Magic Tree House series, by Mary Pope Osborne

The Percy Jackson and the Olympians series, by Rick Riordan

The Phineas L. MacGuire series, by Frances O'Roark Dowell

The Ralph S. Mouse series, by Beverly Cleary

The Ramona series, Beverly Cleary

The Sam series, by Lois Lowry

The Time Warp Trio series, by Jon Scieszka

WHO DONE IT?

Everyone loves a mystery. The desire to find out who did it, what happened, and why they did it keeps the pages turning. The skills you need to solve a mystery—paying attention and looking for clues—are the very skills you need to be a good reader. Being a good reader is being a good detective!

The 39 Clues series, by Rick Riordan

The Boy in the Burning House, by Tim Wynne-Jones

The Cam Jansen series, by David A. Adler

Chasing Vermeer, by Blue Balliett

From the Mixed-Up Files of Mrs. Basil E. Frankweiler, by E. L. Konigsburg

Ghost Canoe, by Will Hobbs

Gaffer Samson's Luck, by Jill Paton Walsh

Nate the Great, by Marjorie Weinman Sharmat

Running Out of Time, by Margaret Peterson Haddix

The Thief Lord, by Cornelia Funke

Tom's Midnight Garden, by Philippa Pearce

Trouble Is My Beeswax, by Bruce Hale

Westing Game, by Ellen Raskin

A Wrinkle in Time, by Madeleine L'Engle

WHAT ARE LITTLE BOYS AND GIRLS MADE OF?

I draw distinctions between girl readers and boy readers with trepidation. Like it or not, gender can make a difference when it comes to what children like to read. Kids need to relate to the stories they meet with characters who provide them with a vision of who they are and who they might become. In a perfect world I want boys and girls reading great stories regardless of the main character's sex, but in the real world, I want children reading, period.

Books with Spirited Boy Protagonists

American Boy: The Adventures of Mark Twain, by Don Brown

Bill Peet: An Autobiography, by Bill Peet

Bully for You, Teddy Roosevelt!, by Jean Fritz

By the Great Horn Spoon!, by Sid Fleischman

Goodnight, Mr. Tom, by Michelle Magorian

The Haymeadow, by Gary Paulsen

The Hero Schliemann: The Dreamer Who Dug for Troy, by Laura Amy Schlitz

Joey Pigza Swallowed the Key, by Jack Gantos

Kokopelli's Flute, by Will Hobbs

Maniac Magee, by Jerry Spinelli

Napoleon, by Robert Burleigh

Odd Boy Out: Young Albert Einstein, by Don Brown

Shiloh, by Phyllis Reynolds Naylor

Books with Spirited Girl Protagonists

Amelia and Eleanor Go for a Ride, by Pam Munoz Ryan

The Double Life of Pocahontas, by Jean Fritz

The Girl with 500 Middle Names, by Margaret Peterson Haddix

Ella Enchanted, by Gail Carson Levine

Hey World, Here I Am!, by Jean Little

Pippi Longstocking, by Astrid Lindgren

Red Scarf Girl, by Ji-Li Jiang

Ronia, the Robber's Daughter, by Astrid Lindgren

They Led the Way, by Johanna Johnston

Ties That Bind, Ties That Break, by Lensey Namioka

What to Do About Alice?, by Barbara Kerley

Wise Child, by Monica Furlong

DRAGONS, GENIES, WIZARDS, AND DAEMONS

*"We were talking of dragons, Tolkien and I in a Berkshire bar. The big workman,
who had sat silent and sucked his pipe all the evening, from his empty mug
with gleaming eyes glanced towards us; 'I seen 'em myself,' he said fiercely."*
—C. S. LEWIS

Fantasy, the struggle and eventual triumph of good over evil, takes us on a journey to a world inhabited by dragons, genies, humans, wizards, and daemons.

The Book of Three, by Lloyd Alexander

The Chronicles of Chrestomanci series, by Diana Wynne Jones

Dark Is Rising, by Susan Cooper

The Dragon of Lonely Island, by Rebecca Rupp

Far-Flung Adventures: Fergus Crane, by Paul Stewart and Chris Riddell

Five Children and It, by E. Nesbit

The Great Tree of Avalon, by T. A. Barron

Half Magic, by Edward Eager

The Lion, the Witch and the Wardrobe, by C. S. Lewis

Redwall, by Brian Jacques

The Spiderwick Chronicles series, by Holly Black and Tony DiTerlizzi

A Wrinkle in Time, by Madeleine L'Engle

"I'M NOBODY! WHO ARE YOU?"

Did you zone out during the six-week unit on poetry? What did the poem mean and what did the sunset represent? Why were you expected to understand all the hidden meanings? Have some empathy for those unfortunate teachers of long ago, who did not have at their disposal all of the wonderful poetry books we have today. Poetry, like music, can take us from misery to hope and joy, from silly to serious, and from bewilderment to astonishment and everywhere in between. Take poetry off the mantle and put a little poetry in your everyday life—it's a vitamin for the spirit.

All the Small Poems and Fourteen More, by Valerie Worth

Comets, Stars, the Moon and Mars: Space Poems and Paintings,
   by Douglas Florian

Falling Up, by Shel Silverstein

Hailstones and Halibut Bones, by Mary O'Neill

Honey, I Love and Other Love Poems, by Eloise Greenfield

Moon, Have You Met My Mother?, by Karla Kuskin

The New Kid on the Block, by Jack Prelutsky

Poetry Speaks to Children, by Elise Paschen

A Poke in the I, by Paul Janeczko

The Random House Book of Poetry for Children, by Jack Prelutsky

Talking Like the Rain, edited by X. J. Kennedy

Technically It's Not My Fault, by John Gradits

HOPEFULLY EVER AFTER

No one has to teach a child to wish; wishing comes naturally. Who hasn't been seduced by a "once upon a time" and "happily ever after"? Who doesn't love to be transported to a place that only exists in the realm of the imagination, where genies and giants and fairy godmothers are there at your beck and call? If you expect "happily ever after" in all these tales you will be pleasantly surprised, and if you think fairy tales can be too predictable, don't miss *The Stinky Cheese Man* and *The Paper Bag Princess*.

The Apple-Pip Princess, by Jane Ray

The Arabian Nights, illustrated by Earle Goodenow

Fairy Tales and Fantastic Stories, by Terry Jones

Fairy Tale Feasts, by Jane Yolen

The Giant Golden Book of Elves and Fairies, by Jane Werner

Goldilocks and the Three Bears, by James Marshall

Lon Po Po: A Red-Riding Hood Story from China, by Ed Young

The Paper Bag Princess, by Robert Munsch

Rumpelstiltskin, by the Brothers Grimm and Paul O. Zelinsky

The Stinky Cheese Man and Other Fairly Stupid Tales, by Jon Scieszka

Fairy Tales from Hans Christian Andersen, by Hans Christian Andersen

Yeh Shen: A Cinderella Story from China, by Ed Young

STORIES PASSED FROM GENERATION TO GENERATION

Folklore is a combination of legend, myth, and folktales that have been passed down from generation to generation. Whether they are told around a campfire, at the kitchen table, or on the lap of a grandparent, these stories encompass a person's hopes, fears, and beliefs. These stories are how people come to understand themselves and the larger world.

American Tall Tales, by Mary Pope Osborne

Can You Guess My Name? Traditional Tales Around the World, by Judy Sierra

Crow and Weasel, by Barry Lopez

Cut from the Same Cloth: American Women of Myth, Legend, and Tall Tale, by Robert D. San Souci

D'Aulaires' Book of Greek Myths, by Ingri and Edgar d'Aulaire

The Jack Tales, by Richard Chase

John Henry, by Julius Lester

The Magical Monkey King: Mischief in Heaven, by Ji-Li Jiang

The Seven Chinese Brothers, by Margaret Mahy

Stories from the Silk Road, retold by Cherry Gilchrist

The People Could Fly: American Black Folktales, by Virginia Hamilton

Thirteen Moons on Turtle's Back, by Joseph Bruchac

The Troll with No Heart in His Body, by Lise Lunge-Larsen

Unwitting Wisdom: An Anthology of Aesop's Fables, by Helen Ward

TWO PAGES OR LESS?

Short stories pack a wallop and give you a bang for your buck. A short story is not all nine innings of a baseball game, but just one—and just maybe, the most exciting inning of the game. To uncover the pleasure in reading short stories, follow the good advice of William Trevor, the master of the short story, who said that if you want to find your way around a short story, read it more than once. Don't speed-read; the riches are found in savoring the stories slowly.

Best Shorts, selected by Avi with Carolyn Shute

The Devil's Storybook, by Natalie Babbitt

Every Living Thing, by Cynthia Rylant

Leaping Beauty, by Gregory Maguire

Necklace of Raindrops, by Joan Aiken

Places I Never Meant to Be, edited by Judy Blume

Rats on the Roof, by James Marshall

Some of the Kinder Planets, by Tim Wynne-Jones

Sweet and Sour, by Carol Kendall and Yao-Wen Li

Tripping Over the Lunch Lady, edited by Nancy E. Mercado

What Do Fish Have to Do With Anything?, by Avi

The Wonder Clock, by Howard Pyle

Zlateh the Goat and Other Stories, by Isaac Bashevis Singer

PICTURE ARE WORDS AND WORDS ARE PICTURES

Graphic novels are attracting loyal fans. Don't assume that graphic novels are just for reluctant readers. They are as demanding, engaging, and creative as any book for children who love stories and storytelling. Good visual storytelling defines the best of this genre, where there is just as much story in the artwork as there is in the words. Novels with illustrations are nothing new but these books offer something new in terms of visuals. Enjoyment of a graphic novel demands that readers don't miss any of the pictorial clues—pay attention as you turn every page. A picture really is worth a thousand words!

The Arrival, by Shaun Tan

Digging Up Dinosaurs, by Aliki

Four Pictures by Emily Carr, by Nicolas Debon

Good Masters! Sweet Ladies!, by Laura Amy Schlitz

Houdini: The Handcuff King, by Jason Lutes

Laika, by Nick Abadzis

The Legend of Hong Kil Dong: The Robin Hood of Korea,
    by Anne Sibley O'Brien

Rapunzel's Revenge, by Shannon Hale and Dean Hale

Robot Dreams, by Sara Varon

Satchel Paige: Striking Out Jim Crow, by James Sturm and Rich Tommaso

Simon's Dream, by Susan Schade and John Buller

The Strongest Man in the World, by Nicolas Debon

There's a Wolf at the Door, by Zoe B. Alley

The Wall: Growing Up Behind the Iron Curtain, by Peter Sís

SWEEP—JUST DON'T SWEEP IT UNDER THE RUG

Some conversations are more difficult than others, but don't let that translate into not having the conversation. Children need adults who are willing to talk about hard subjects. A willingness to take a subject out of the dark, expose it to the light of day, and let go of the need to arrive at a solution makes for an important conversation everyone can begin. Include books on these subjects—such as death, illness, and divorce—in your child's repertoire, before you *need* the conversation. Books shed light on difficult subjects and allow children to know they are not alone. So, when you meet a book on a difficult subject, remember that conversations are not just about finding solutions and solving problems.

Dear Mr. Henshaw, by Beverly Cleary

Each Little Bird That Sings, by Deborah Wiles

Lifetimes, by Bryan Mellonie

Mick Harte Was Here, by Barbara Park

Missing May, by Cynthia Rylant

Now One Foot, Now the Other, by Tomie de Paola

Ola's Wake, by B. J. Stone

One Small Dog, by Joanna Hurwitz

Rudi's Pond, by Eve Bunting

Sadako and the Thousand Paper Cranes, by Eleanor Coerr

Six Innings, by James Preller

Tear Soup, by Pat Schweibert

This Place I Know: Poems of Comfort, selected by Georgia Heard

MONEY DOESN'T GROW ON TREES

You want to go to Hawaii for vacation, your son wants a new soccer jersey, and your daughter wants private skiing lessons—all of this adds up. As parents you want to instill good financial values, regardless of your income level. Talking about money isn't always easy. Do you give your children an allowance? How much is too much? Do they know the word *budget*? It's never too early to teach your children that money doesn't grow on trees.

26 Letters and 99 Cents, by Tana Hoban

Allowance Magic: Turn Your Kids into Money Wizards, by David McCurrach

The Berenstain Bears' Trouble with Money, by Stan and Jan Berenstain

The Everything Kids' Money Book, by Diane Mayr

Money Sense for Kids, by Hollis Page Harman

Raising Financially Fit Kids, by Joline Godfrey

Raising Money Smart Kids, by Janet Bodnar

The Toothpaste Millionaire, by Jean Merrill

OUR INSIDES, AND THE BIRDS AND THE BEES

It's always best to understand the questions your child is asking. This piece of advice reminds me of a story where a little boy asked his mom where he came from. Taking a deep breath she proceeded to talk about plumbing and the birds and the bees. After a few minutes her son interrupted her and said, "Mom, I asked you where I came from—Toledo or Chicago?" Although answering these questions can sometimes be awkward, children just want to know the facts. Here are some books about our bodies, as well as the birds and the bees:

Care and Keeping of You: The Body Book for Girls, by Valorie Schaefer

First Human Body Encyclopedia, by DK Publishing

From Head to Toe: The Amazing Human Body and How It Works,
   by Barbara Seuling

It's Perfectly Normal, by Robie H. Harris and Michael Emberley

It's So Amazing, by Robie H. Harris and Michael Emberley

It's Not the Stork, by Robie H. Harris and Michael Emberley

Jessica's X-Ray, by Pat Zonta

Mommy Laid an Egg: Or, Where Do Babies Come From?, by Babette Cole

The Way We Work, by David Macaulay

HOPE

Parents want their children to feel safe, but traumas, natural disasters, wars, the Holocaust, and racism are all part of the world. The urge is not to talk with children about subjects that are difficult, but the reality is that your children will learn about these subjects, and if not from you, then from someone else. And that "someone else" is not going to have the conversation you want to have with your child. These stories offer a glimpse of both the best and the worst of human nature and put events into a larger context, allowing you to have a more meaningful conversation.

*Freedom Riders: John Lewis and Jim Awerg on the Front Lines of the
   Civil Rights Movement*, by Ann Aausum

Iqbal, by Francesco D'Adamo

Never to Forget: The Jews of the Holocaust, by Milton Meltzer

Night of the Twisters, by Ivy Ruckman

Number the Stars, by Lois Lowry

Rescue: The Story of How Gentiles Saved Jews in the Holocaust, by Milton Meltzer

Sadako and the Thousand Paper Cranes, by Eleanor Coerr

Stone Goddess, by Minfong Ho

Terrible Things, by Eve Bunting

This Place I Know: Poems of Comfort, selected by Georgia Heard

Twenty and Ten, by Claire Huchet Bishop

The Wall, by Eve Bunting

The War Prayer, by Mark Twain

The Watsons Go to Birmingham—1963, by Christopher Paul Curtis

THEY THINK THEY KNOW EVERYTHING

Adolescents create and re-create themselves on a daily basis as they search for their identity. The desire to be noticed, to be invisible, to be grown up, to be a child—life can be complicated! Richard Peck nailed adolescents when he said they are as impressionable as wet cement. Adolescence is a time of beginning to figure out who you are and finding your place in the world. This is also a time when parents ask what happened to their delightful and lovable child of not so long ago. These books are invaluable reads for parents and children because what these books have in common is their refreshing honesty about the way real people grow into genuine adulthood. From grade 6 to 8+ there is a window of opportunity to hand your adolescent child the books that will carry them into high school. These are some of my favorite books to meet before high school but not before sixth grade.

The Chocolate War, by Robert Cormier

The Contender, by Robert Lipsyte

Fahrenheit 451, by Ray Bradbury

Flour Babies, by Anne Fine

The Goats, by Brock Cole

The Gospel According to Larry, by Janet Tashjian

Make Lemonade, by Virginia Euwer Wolff

Nothing But the Truth, by Avi

Past Perfect, Present Tense, by Richard Peck

Speak, by Laurie Halse Anderson

Stargirl, by Jerry Spinelli

Staying Fat for Sarah Brynes, by Chris Crutcher

MIXED NUTS

Some books just don't cooperate and won't allow themselves to be categorized; they are as varied as a bowl of mixed nuts. Some of them will stretch your imagination, some of them will amuse you, some of them will encourage you to "play" with them, but *all* of them will delight you.

A Chocolate Moose for Dinner, by Fred Gwynne

Alexander and the Terrible, Horrible, No Good, Very Bad Day, by Judith Viorst

CDB!, by William Steig

Creative Whack Pack, by Roger Von Oech

Go Hang a Salami! I'm a Lasagna Hog!: and Other Palindromes, by John Agee

Look-Alikes, by Joan Steiner

Opposites, More Opposites, and a Few Differences, by Richard Wilbur

The Shrinking of Treehorn, by Florence Parry Heide

Shortcut, by David Macaulay

Stories to Solve, by George Shannon

Stormy Night, by Michèle Lemieux

True Lies, by George Shannon

Voices in the Park, by Anthony Browne

HOME-RUN BOOKS

Abraham Lincoln said, "My best friend is a person who will give me a book I have not read." Create a list of your favorite books and become someone's best friend by giving them a book they have not read. Start your lists and share them—you can even send me a copy!

1. _____

2. _____

3. _____

4. _____

5. _____

6. _____

7. _____

8. _____

9. _____

10. _____

★ ★ ★ Don't stop with 10!

Acknowledgments

I have spent the last twenty years in the company of some of the most generous individuals you could ever hope to meet—parents, teachers, librarians, school administrators, and, last but not least, independent booksellers—who all share the goal of making sure children love reading and are reading quality books.

Thank you to:

> **Parents** who take my classes and workshops and provide valuable information on the reading habits of their children and who give me feedback on the conversations the books generate. I learn something valuable from every parent.

> **Faculty** who graciously allow me inside their classrooms to work with their students. I love working with teachers in creating dynamic classroom discussions and helping students discover the excitement of reading and talking about books.

> **School administrators** whose foresight and generosity make parent education a top priority.

> **School librarians.** What a privilege to be part of creating vibrant school libraries.

I don't have the space to mention all the wonderful people I have met internationally but my work with them has reinforced my understanding of how every culture values the importance of children learning to be good readers. My special thanks go to Yolanda Yeh, managing director of Pro-Active Learning. Yolanda's vision and deep commitment to the educational life for children in Hong Kong is admirable, and I am profoundly grateful that I have had the opportunity to work with her, doing workshops for schools, parents, and various organizations.

I owe a big thank-you to Benjamin Franklin who was instrumental in bringing about the public library as we know it today. I fell in love with libraries as a child and the love affair lives on. The next best thing to libraries are independent bookstores. I am lucky to have met Bonnie Stuppin at Alexander Book Company in San Francisco. Thank you, Bonnie, for your bountiful knowledge, friendship, and support.

I first met my literary agent, Kitty Cowles, in one of my classes. Kitty experienced firsthand the benefits of having conversations with her daughter, Carson, on the books we read in class. I am grateful for her vision and her encouragement in making *Reading Together* a reality.

My editor, Meg Leder, with her love of children's literature and enthusiasm for *Reading Together*, made all the difference. Thank you, Meg. A heartfelt thank-you to all the behind-the-scene people at Perigee—publisher John Duff, sales and marketing director Patrick Nolan, managing editor Jennifer Eck, and publicist Kaitlyn Kennedy.

A special thank-you goes to Cathleen O'Brien. Following years of reading and talking with children, parents, and teachers about stories, I realized there were some unexpected challenges in taking those conversations and committing them to paper. Cathleen became the "conversational buddy" I needed to write good questions that would jump-start conversations. Cathleen took every question to heartand I was impressed with the integrity she brought to each conversation. I am enormously appreciative for her wisdom, her generosity of spirit, and her humor.

At the end of the day, I feel so fortunate for the opportunities I have to influence the reading habits of children. *Reading Together* would not have been possible without the love and support I receive from my family, friends, and acquaintances. A special thank-you to Isa—for her love and support and for all the little things she does that make my work possible. To my husband, George, and my sons, Daniel and Toby—I thank each of you from the bottom of my heart. Love—forever and a day.

Index

Page numbers in **bold** represent Story Pages.

INDEX

INDEX

About the Author

Diane W. Frankenstein, who holds a master's degree in children's literature and language arts from San Francisco State University, has been an educational consultant in children's and adolescent literature since 1989. She works throughout the United States as well as in Asia and Europe. Diane is married with two sons and lives in San Francisco. She is trying to figure out how to read every book in the Library of Congress and still keep a homemade chicken soup warm on the stove. Visit her website at www.dianefrankenstein.com.